The Origins of Intellect

1.882

SECOND EDITION

The Origins of
Intellect
Piaget's Theory

John L. Phillips, Jr.
BOISE STATE UNIVERSITY

W. H. Freeman and Company
San Francisco

Library of Congress Cataloging in Publication Data

Phillips, John L.   1923–
    The origins of intellect.

    Bibliography: p.
    Includes index.
    1. Intellect.   2. Child study.   3. Piaget,
Jean, 1896–   I. Title
BF431.P47 1975   155.4'13   75-5703
ISBN 0-7167-0579-6
ISBN 0-7167-0580-X pbk.

Printed in the United States of America

    4 5 6 7 8 9 10

To Greg and Jeff

Contents

Preface to the
Second Edition

The first edition of this book was exceedingly well received. Why change it?

Piaget's theory has not changed fundamentally in the five years since the manuscript for that edition was completed, but new efforts have been made to make practical use of the theory in education. So, although it may be a case of the tail wagging the dog, it is because of those educational experiments that a revision was undertaken.

Once it *was* undertaken, however, I saw the revision as an opportunity to improve the theoretical chapters as well. I read carefully all published reviews of the book and solicited suggestions from a randomly selected sample of professors who had used it. I also plunged more deeply into the Piagetian literature than I ever had before. The result is a relatively minor revision of the theoretical chapters.

The outline of stages is different—four major "periods" instead of three. I have changed it because everyone, including Piaget, keeps referring to four stages. I have made the change reluctantly, because I discern relatively well-equilibrated action systems at the ends of the Sensorimotor Period, the Concrete Operations Period, and the Formal Operations Period. Pre-operational thinking, in my view, is just what its name implies— a transition into concrete operational thinking. But there are other views, and it *is* easier to talk about four periods than about three with one divided into subperiods. In any case, students should be prepared for the terminology that is currently being used. "Schema" was changed to "scheme" for the same reason.

There are new sections on "Equilibration," "Factors in Development," "Imitation in the Service of Play," "Coordination of Assimilation and Accommodation," and "Egocentricity in Reasoning"; but except for them and a few substantive refinements in other sections, most of the many changes are linguistic.

Two new features have been added for the convenience of the reader: (1) page numbers appear in the table of contents that precedes each chapter as a supplement to the general table of contents at the front of the book and the index at the back; and (2) the source notes have been placed at the end of each chapter, with entries keyed to the text by number. The latter feature allows a reader to investigate any of those references, but it also allows him to ignore them if he chooses. Explanatory notes are retained at the foot of the page.

Once again I have been assisted in many ways by many people. Scholars who helped include Jerome Bruner, Tim Collias, Marjorie Crutchfield, Edward M. Docherty, Jr., J. A. Easley, Jr., John H. Flavell, Hans G. Furth, Walter E. Hathaway, Richard L. Kimball, Jonas Langer, Edward G. Meyers, Gary Newby, Patricia Nolen, June B. Pimm, Adrien Pinard, Robert Ross, L. L. Stewin, Eunice Wallace, David Weikert, and Burton White.

Special thanks are due Constance Kamii and John Renner, whose work is described at length in the chapter on educational implications of the theory. They are not responsible for the interpretations that appear there; but their correspondence was generous and helpful, and I am grateful to them for it.

The library staff at Boise State University has been gracious and efficient as always; and my wife, Elaine, who did the secretarial work, has been patient when things were moving slowly and industrious when they were moving fast. Together, we discovered that if an author is conscientious, revising a book is a lot of work!

March 1975   *John L. Phillips, Jr.*

Preface to the
First Edition

TO THE TEACHER

When, just a few years ago, I was given the responsibility of planning a course in educational psychology, I very quickly made two decisions: (1) that it would be a course in psychology, not pedagogical methods, and (2) that it would have some focus.

I was surprised and delighted to find both the psychology and the focus in a collection of works that had been around for a long time. I had heard of Piaget, of course, for many years; but earlier, those who referred to him at all always did so with more than a modicum of condescending tolerance. Recently, however, I have detected a cognitive trend in the literature: more American psychologists have been directing their search for a theoretical model away from the laboratory rat and toward the electronic computer. I also discovered that many more writers are interested in Piaget and that most of their references to him are suffused with respect.

Consequently, I made an intensive study of Piaget; this book is the result of that study. It was originally a set of notes designed for use in teaching a class of upper-division students in educational psychology. The class was small enough to allow student participation, and my plan was to involve them as much as possible in the theoretical enterprise. It is not possible, of course, to do that in a book to the same extent that it can be done in a classroom, but the style of this book still reflects my original purpose. Often a problem is stated, and then the student is invited to think it through, using the same data as were available to Piaget. Many actual observations are reported in order to make that feasible.

Beyond that, this book is a general summary, at a relatively nontechnical level, of Piaget's theory of the development of intelligence. It should serve very well the busy teacher of child psychology, child development, or educational psychology; of learning or psychological systems; or perhaps even of general psychology.

The book is *not* intended to be *The Compleat Piaget*. What I have done is to present Piaget's original theory together with enough illustrations of his research activities to give the theory meaning. The theory has only recently caught the interest of more than a few American psychologists; but it was actually promulgated many years ago, and although Piaget has refined his theoretical models and, along with others at Geneva and elsewhere, has produced more recent research than is included here, the basic theory remains essentially the same and can be presented most clearly in the context of its original development. Readers who have mastered these theoretical rudiments and wish to progress further will find an excellent review of Piaget's recent work, as well as a more thorough (and also more technical) discussion of the theory itself, plus a review of the studies of perception and moral concepts, in J. H. Flavell's *The Developmental Psychology of Jean Piaget* (1963).

Probably every teacher will have his own way of beginning the study of intellectual development in general and of Piaget's work in particular. My own way is to introduce my students to the theory of D. O. Hebb, because they have been encouraged to

take a naturalistic view of human behavior, and because I believe that Hebb has successfully demonstrated how—in principle,
at least—"the ghost in the machine" can be dealt with in naturalistic terms. If the theoretical foundations of your course are
cognitive to begin with, that will be of no concern to you, but
I have felt the need of a bridge between the S-R paradigm with
which I begin my course and the cognitive system that is Piaget.
If you should feel the same need, you could put a Hebb book on
reserve in your library: *A Textbook of Psychology* if your students
are in teacher training, *The Organization of Behavior* if they are
psychology majors. (The first edition of the *Textbook* is really
better for your purpose than the second, in my opinion.)

The Origins of Intellect will serve nicely as a self-contained
exposition of Piaget's theory. However, if you should wish to
make that theory (and its practical implications) a substantial
part of your course, you will want your students also to discuss
it during class periods and perhaps to work with it outside of
class. Often a greater involvement of students in the working
through of scientific ideas can be fostered by supplementing
their reading with graphic demonstrations of the tests of those
ideas. As of this date I know of no suitable films of Piagetian
tests, but there is a supply of subjects in nearly every community,
and for demonstration purposes, students can administer the
tests themselves. I usually assign at least one observation at each
of three levels: Sensorimotor, Preoperational, and Concrete
Operations. (The Formal Operations test described in the book
requires more equipment than can be quickly and easily assembled by every student.) When making these assignments, students
should be reminded that the most interesting results of the
Piaget-type tests are the failures that occur; you might suggest
that for each subject they try to find one test that he passes and
one that he fails. And tell them to use each situation to learn as
much as possible about the structure of the child's thought.
They will find that they do indeed learn more from the failures
than from the successes.

As a sequel to the unit on Piaget, two paperback volumes by
Jerome Bruner seem to me especially appropriate: *The Process
of Education* and *Toward a Theory of Instruction*. A careful examina-

tion of the journal articles cited in my bibliography will reveal an even more recent interest in the application of ideas similar to those of Piaget to problems in education. I was recently privileged to hear Robert M. Gagné's presidential address to Division 15 of the American Psychological Association. It was a paper entitled "Learning Hierarchies," which could, if one were so inclined, be used to explore my suggestion in Chapter V that a more thorough task analysis may be an avenue to progress in the teaching of operations. That paper has not been published, but the bibliography includes others that have. In this regard, I should mention that some articles have been reprinted in edited collections and that only a few of those are listed here with their original sources. The edited collections are rich mines of source materials.

TO THE STUDENT

The chapter that I have called "Introduction" is primarily a quick survey of Piaget's entire theory, in preparation for a more detailed analysis of its parts. Very little of that chapter describes my approach to the teaching of the theory or relates it to the motivations of students. The following remarks are intended to remedy that omission.

SPECIAL FEATURES AND STUDY SUGGESTIONS

Because it is so often useful to make comparisons of one stage of development with another, I have continually sought opportunities for juxtaposition; so each topic heading refers to a sort of *mode* rather than to an exclusive category—e.g., in the section on Concrete Operations, much is said about Preoperational thinking in order that the differences between the two might be made clear. This means that the length of a section does not indicate very precisely the amount of attention that has been given to the topic announced in its heading; it means, too, that not all information pertinent to an announced topic may be found under that particular heading. But the comparison technique does build concepts efficiently, and that, after all, is our major objective.

In order to make the most of those conceptual acquisitions, you must weave them into a coherent pattern. It is the function of Chapter 1 to help you do just that. You are likely to find Chapter 1 exceedingly difficult the first time through, and it probably will not be very helpful by itself. But because the concepts introduced there are illustrated later on, the chapter can perform an organizing function if you will use it properly. A lecturer, of course, has more control of his students than an author does, and one of the ways in which I exercised that control when I was lecturing was to require, at the end of what is now Chapter 5,* a careful review of Chapter 1, so that the latter might serve as both an introduction to the theory and a summary of it. It is a difficult theory, and you will find Chapter 1 only vaguely intelligible on first reading; but I have presented it in the only intellectually honest way I could conceive, and the difficulty that you may have with it initially should heighten your satisfaction in the understanding that will be yours on the second try. The procedure that I recommend, and which has proven effective in my own classes, is as follows:

1. Read Chapter 1 with a set to remember where each topic is discussed (rather than for mastery of content).
2. Refer back to parts of it as you go through the other sections, this time digesting the content.
3. Reread the entire chapter after you have completed Chapter 5 and before you begin Chapter 6, striving now for an understanding of broad general relationships.

PIAGET AND PSYCHOLOGY

As you complete Chapters 2 through 5 and return for a review of Chapter 1, a pattern will emerge, and you will comprehend better than you had at first my reasons for referring to "intelli-

---

*In this reprinted Preface, all chapter numbers have been adjusted to agree with the new numbering of chapters.

gence" as "the efficient processing of information" and for pointing out the compatibility of Piaget's system with Hebb's neurological theory. The lecture materials were selected and organized in this way because my reading of the literature reveals a marked increase in the amount of attention that psychologists have been giving recently to central mediating processes, and because my own interest has been moving in that direction. The change is epitomized by the choice of models in psychological theory. A shift seems to be occurring from stimulus-response connections to feedback loops—from the laboratory rat to the electronic computer.

My point about the shift from rat to computer is not that we have built computers more complex than the nervous system of a rat, but rather that in principle we *could* do so and, more important perhaps, that the programming of a computer demands a thorough analysis of the central organizing processes that control output—which, according to this view, is what psychology is all about. I hope that you will take from all this a conception of the human brain as a vastly complicated system for the storage, retrieval, and organization of information; a system that becomes more complex as it operates, and hence becomes capable of increasingly complex operations; a system that changes in ways that are at least to some degree similar to the constructions that Piaget has given us.

REFERENCE BY FUTURE WRITERS

The publications of the Geneva school constitute by far the largest repository of knowledge about the cognitive development of children that is available anywhere; students of psychology should be familiar with Piaget's theory even if it turns out to be basically wrong, because it will undoubtedly serve as a base for many future studies of children's thinking.

UNDERSTANDING FOR ITS OWN SAKE

If Piaget is correct, understanding is reinforcing in and of itself. If so, your study of this book should be rewarded not only by its effect on your subsequent reading about children, but more directly by its effect on your interaction with them. You should experience a satisfaction similar to that of an anthropologist who has been studying a preliterate culture and, after much intensive effort, develops the ability to see the world as the natives do, and thus at last really to communicate with them.

PRACTICAL IMPLICATIONS

Satisfactions of that kind should be sufficient unto themselves—particularly for people who will be in daily contact with children; but if you are a prospective teacher, counselor, or school psychologist, you are doubtless eager to find additional rewards related to your professional activities.

If you were to review the first five chapters with that in mind, you might very well find for yourself some important implications of the theory for educators in general and teachers in particular. Your review time, however, might better be spent in a concentrated effort to understand the theory as such. After you have done that, you will be ready to consider in Chapter 6 some of the implications of the theory for those who would intervene in the developmental process.

December 1968   *John L. Phillips, Jr.*

The Origins of Intellect

Introduction

Introduction

Despite the clear implication of its title, this chapter is not the beginning of the book. It begins on page xv in the Preface to the First Edition.

It is true that a preface always contains some information that is of no interest to most readers, but the Preface is more important in this book than in most. It explains the structure of the book, and that structure is essential to efficient study of the main body of the text.

PIAGET AND HIS METHODS

Jean Piaget* is a Swiss psychologist who was trained in zoology and whose major interests are essentially philosophical. He and his associates have been publishing their findings on the development of cognitive processes in children since 1927, and have

---

*Pronounced *Pyasey: ya* as in "yak," *s* as in "pleasure," and *ey* as in "they." That's easy to say, and it is very close to the original French; so just about everyone does it that way. Unfortunately, no such consensus has emerged

accumulated the largest store of factual and theoretical observations extant today.

Piaget is often criticized because his method of investigation, though somewhat modified in recent years, is still largely clinical. He observes the child's surroundings and his behavior, formulates a hypothesis concerning the structure that underlies and includes them both, and then tests that hypothesis by altering the surroundings slightly—by rearranging the materials, by posing the problem in a different way, or even by overtly suggesting to the subject a response different from the one predicted by the theory.

An example of the method is the investigation of the preoperational child's conception of velocity. The child observes the movement of an object through points A, B, C, and D. He reports that the object passed through point D "after" point A and that it took "more time" to get from A to C than from A to B. From this it might reasonably be inferred that the child's conception of temporal succession and duration is the same as that of an adult. But the investigation doesn't stop there. The subject is then presented with the simultaneous movements of *two* objects. The investigator systematically varies the actual distance through which each of the objects moves, their times in transit, and their initial and terminal positions relative to one another. When that is done, the child no longer responds as an adult would in similar circumstances. For example, if two objects move simultaneously—i.e., if they start simultaneously and stop simultaneously—but at different velocities, the child will deny their simultaneity of movement. To him, each moving object has a different "time"—a time that is a function of the *spatial* features of the display.

The systematic manipulation of variables illustrated by that example is certainly in the tradition of classical experimental

concerning the adjective, "Piagetian." Because English nouns ending in "et" do not have a silent "t," there is no rule for the pronunciation of the adjectival form of such a noun. Consequently one hears many different versions of "Piagetian." The most graceful of them, in my opinion, simply adds "shun" to the now standard pronunciation of "Piaget."

science. The example, however, is drawn from one of the more rigorous of the studies done by Piaget and his colleagues. Their investigations often begin with naturalistic observations and continue as an interaction between the child and the "experimenter"—an interaction in which each varies his own behavior in response to that of the other.

Another example may serve to illustrate the point: it is an "experiment" designed to reveal the child's conception of number. The child is presented with an assemblage of coins and a large number of flowers; he is asked to tell how many flowers he can purchase with the coins if the price of each flower is one coin. Here is a transcript of one such encounter:

> Gui (four years, four months) put 5 flowers opposite 6 pennies, then made a one-for-one exchange of 6 pennies for 6 flowers (taking the extra flower from the reserve supply). The pennies were in a row and the flowers bunched together: "What have we done?— *We've exchanged them.*—Then is there the same number of flowers and pennies?—*No.*—Are there more on one side?—*Yes.*—Where?— *There* (pennies). (The exchange was again made, but this time the pennies were put in a pile and the flowers in a row.) Is there the same number of flowers and pennies?—*No.*—Where are there more?—*Here* (flowers).— And here (pennies)?—*Less.*[1]

This shifting of experimental procedures to fit the responses of a particular subject makes replication difficult, and the results may be especially susceptible to the "experimenter effect."* The reader who feels impelled to criticize Piaget's method is in good company. But before becoming too enthusiastic a critic, he should be sure to note the deliberate effort that is made to give

---

*Sometimes called the "Rosenthal effect," after R. Rosenthal, who in several recent studies has demonstrated that even in apparently objective experimental situations, the experimenter can influence the subject's behavior in a number of subtle and unacknowledged ways (facial expression, tone of voice, etc.). Even rat subjects perform better for experimenters who expect them to do so, presumably because of differences in handling by different experimenters.[3]

the child opportunities for responses that would *not* fit the theory. He should also keep in mind Piaget's epistemological position that knowledge is action (though not necessarily motor action). The subject is continually acting. His actions are structured, and they are also to some extent autonomous. The investigator must therefore continually change his line of attack if he is to follow those actions and to discern their underlying structure. Indeed, since that structure does differ from child to child, the investigator may find it necessary at times to vary his language when posing a problem in order to ensure that the problem *will* be the same for different children. Rigidly standardized procedures might defeat the very purpose for which they were designed, because their meanings vary from one subject to another. The important thing is to "make contact with the child's thinking."[2]

RELATION TO AMERICAN PSYCHOLOGY

The early work of Piaget's Geneva group was given considerable attention in the scholarly press, but because psychology, especially in the United States, was at that time dominated by associationistic theories of learning and by content-oriented psychometrics, their work generated little interest.

The current explosion of interest in Piaget's work is an expression of the same concern that has produced conceptions of man as a rule-formulating, rule-following organism and of his brain as an incredibly complex organic system for processing information. That concern may have resulted not only from a dissatisfaction with existing theories but also from advances that have taken place recently in neurophysiology and computer engineering.

In any case, Piaget's observations and formulations are today a definite focus of theoretical and professional interest in psychology. The theory is cognitive rather than associationistic,* it

---

*A cognitive theory is concerned especially with central organizing processes in higher animals, and it recognizes a partial autonomy of those processes, such that the animal becomes an actor upon, rather than simply a reactor to

is concerned primarily with structure rather than content—with *how* the mind works rather than with *what* it does. It is concerned more with understanding than with prediction and control of behavior.

These remarks can of course be made only by way of emphasis, for we can never know the *how* except through the *what*; we can only infer central processes from the behaviors that they organize. An affirmation of one kind of analysis does not necessarily imply a negation of the other. There are conflicts between them, but often the dissonance is more apparent than real, and a careful reading of both kinds of analysis reveals a harmony that could not be seen at first glance. In this book, discussion of Piaget's theory is written only partly in the idiom of Piaget. "Input," "output," and "feedback," for example, are less-than-lyrical words that American psychologists have borrowed from engineering. Piaget does without them, but we shall find them useful. Even the term "learning" appears very seldom in Piaget's writings, and when it does, it is nearly always accompanied by a modifier. Conditioning, whether classical or instrumental, respondent or operant, he calls "learning in the narrow sense"; changes in cognitive structure are referred to not as learning but as "development." In this book, we shall use both the Piagetian and the more standard psychological terms and attempt to understand how they all relate to Piaget's ideas.

One more thing should be said about his system in relation to others. Piaget's early academic training was in zoology, and his theory of cognitive development is rooted firmly there. That, coupled with the feature of invariant stages, has caused some writers to label the theory "nativist," as though it were holding the child's genetic program responsible for the organization of

---

its environment. Actually, the opposite of all this, the so-called associationist doctrine, is to some extent a straw man; for, excepting B. F. Skinner, who abjures all theories, there is probably no prominent psychologist today who does not explicitly recognize the importance of mediating processes. But there is a difference in emphasis, and like most straw men this one serves the purpose of accentuating that difference.

his behavior. But Piaget's is not a nativist theory. A radical alternative to nativism is "empiricism," the doctrine that behavior is determined by the environment—by reinforcement contingencies and the like. But the theory is not empiricist, either. It has properly been called "interactionist" and "constructivist": the organism *inherits* a genetic program that gradually (through a process called "maturation") provides the biological equipment necessary for *constructing* a stable internal structure out of its experiences with its *environment*. Paradoxically, that stable structure—that "intelligence"—then helps the organism adapt to *changes* in that environment. Our discussions of assimilation, accommodation, and equilibration will attempt to resolve the paradox.

Before turning to the first of the Piagetian periods of development, let us take a quick overview of the theory, in preparation for the more detailed account that will follow in Chapters 2 through 5.

EVOLUTIONARY PERSPECTIVE

The evolution of complex organisms has necessarily been accompanied by that of complex behavioral control systems. A one-celled animal reacts in a severely limited way to its immediate environment; a higher animal has an elaborate repertory of responses to a wide variety of stimuli. But that elaboration and that flexibility are achieved at the expense of biological simplicity; such an animal is composed of many parts—some specialized for reception of information from the environment, others for actions upon it. If it is to adapt successfully to its environment, the higher animal, therefore, must possess a transmission device that integrates the activities of the parts. And of course if it is to survive, the animal *must* adapt.

But once a transmission system has developed, the way is open to the development of alternative arrangements of that system. Thus, not only are the higher animal's reception and response capabilities complex, but so are the mechanisms that relate those capabilities; relations between stimulus and response are different for higher and lower animals. A lower animal is "sense-dominated"; its response to a specific input from the environment is immediate and predictable. A higher animal's behavior, however, is controlled not only by inputs from its immediate surroundings, but also by mediating processes within the transmission system—processes that are partly the result of previous functioning of the system. Therefore, the higher animal's overt response to a specific input is not necessarily immediate, and it is not predictable merely from knowledge of the current input pattern. To predict the behavior of a higher animal, it is necessary to know something about its mediating processes. In order to predict a human subject's response to a combination of digits—say "8" and "2"—I would have to know what he had learned about arithmetic before he ever came into my laboratory; whether he had in the immediate past been instructed to add, to subtract, to multiply, or to divide; whether he had a generalized set to follow directions; and so on. A person's behavior is determined both by the sensory input at the moment and by the way in which his system of mediating processes has been organized.[4]

The twin consequences of sensory and motor differentiations and of the organization of mediating processes are (1) the extension—both spatially and temporally—of the world with which the organism can interact and (2) the freedom to *choose* from among many possible actions. "Intelligence" is the ability to make adaptive choices.

STRUCTURE AND FUNCTION

Adaptation is a biological function. As a child develops, *functions* remain invariant, but *structures* change systematically. Change in structures *is* "development."

Another term found often in Piaget's writings is *content*, by which he means observable stimuli and responses. We may talk in abstract terms about "function" and "structure," but as soon as we cite an actual example, we must deal also with content.

Such an example might be: "A baby looks at a rattle and picks it up." The structure of that event relates the means (looking, reaching, grasping) to the end (stimulation from the object in hand). Each of those is related thereby to the other, and it is that relatedness that Piaget calls "structure."* The function of the baby's act is *adaptation*—i.e., the assimilation of inputs and the accommodation of each element to the others. "Content" refers to the input and output—the raw data of the event, as distinguished from its pattern. The term "structure," on the other hand, refers to the systemic properties of an event; it encompasses all aspects of an act, both internal and external.

Finally, "function" refers to biologically inherited modes of interacting with the environment—modes that are characteristic of such integrations in all biological systems. With reference to intelligence, that inherited "functional nucleus" imposes "certain necessary and irreducible conditions"[5] on structures. Discontinuities in structure arise out of the continuous action of invariant functions. Throughout the developmental period, functions are permanent, but structures are transitory; if they weren't, there would be no development.

There are two basic functions: *adaptation* ("the accord of thought with things"[6]) and *organization* ("the accord of thought with itself"[7]). Adaptation, in turn, consists of *assimilation* and *accommodation*.

ASSIMILATION

If we think of the human brain as an organic machine for processing information, we must realize not only that it is an exceedingly complex machine, but also that its internal structure is continually changing. We must realize also that the precise pattern of cortical activity initiated by an incoming stimulus is a

*See pages 11 and 12.

function not only of the pattern of the stimulus, but also of the way in which the brain has been programmed to deal with it.

Assimilation occurs whenever an organism utilizes something from its environment and incorporates it. A biological example would be the ingestion of food. The food is changed in the process, and so is the organism. Psychological processes are similar in that the pattern in the stimulation is changed and, again, so is the organism.

In introductory psychology courses it is demonstrated that even the perception of an object is not a faithful reproduction of a stimulus pattern. For example, our perception of an object remains the same even though changes in distance, angle of view, and amount of light produce rather striking differences in the size, shape, brightness, and hue of the image that is actually projected onto the retina. (This is, of course, the phenomenon known as "object constancy.") Beyond that, objects are invested with meaning—i.e., they are categorized in terms of such dimensions as familiarity, threat, and beauty. In sum, the input is changed to fit the existing structures. The organism is always active, and its cognitions—even its perceptions of its immediate surroundings—are as much a function of that activity as they are of the physical properties of the environment.

ACCOMMODATION

But at the same time that the input is being changed by the structures, the structures are being changed by the input. For example, object constancy, which was just used to illustrate the former process, can also be used to illustrate the latter. Each "correction" that is applied by the brain to a retinal image had to be learned—i.e., the structures that act upon the input have themselves been shaped by that input.

Take size constancy, for example. Think of the thousands upon thousands of times that the size of an image on your own retina has covaried with distance from you to the object. Many other inputs, such as proprioceptive ones that arise as you have approached the object, and the temporal relations among them, have contributed to the changing patterns of mediation.* The mechanism by which those changes occur Piaget calls "accommodation."

FUNCTIONAL INVARIANTS: ASSIMILATION AND ACCOMMODATION

Accommodation and assimilation are called "functional invariants" because they are characteristic of all biological systems, regardless of the varying contents of those systems. They are not, however, always in balance, one with the other.

Temporary imbalances occur when a child is imitating (accommodation over assimilation) and when he is playing (assimilation over accommodation). Behavior is most adaptive when accommodation and assimilation are in balance; but such a balance is always temporary, because the process of adaptation reveals imperfections in the system. (See the section below on *Equilibration.*)

SCHEMES

As I mentioned previously, cognitive development consists of a succession of changes, and the changes are structural.

Piaget often refers to individual structures as *schemes*. A scheme is a kind of mini-system; it is that property of an action which can be generalized to other contents. For example, the baby who "looks at a *rattle* and picks it up" (p. 9) can do the same with *any* small, lightweight object; i.e., the "look-and-pickup" scheme can assimilate a wide variety of objects—with some accommodations, of course.

Actually, a scheme includes also the stimuli that trigger the mediating processes and the overt behavior that presumably is

---

*There is evidence that some of this organization is either innate or learned very early (before the age of 8 weeks). If learned, it therefore cannot be *via* extensive movement of the infant's body through space. [8]

organized by them. And there can be interactions among schemes; i.e., they can assimilate each other. A "scheme" is a generic unit of structure; "whatever is repeatable or generalizable" is a scheme.[9] The earliest structures are relatively simple; they usually are referred to as "reflexes." Later schemes are more complex—more "mental"—and it becomes increasingly appropriate to think of them as "strategies," "plans," "transformation rules," "expectancies," etc. Whatever their labels, they form a kind of framework onto which incoming sensory data can fit—indeed must fit if they are to have any effect; but it is a framework that is continually changing its shape so that as many data as possible *will* fit.

Figure 1.1 summarizes some of these relationships.

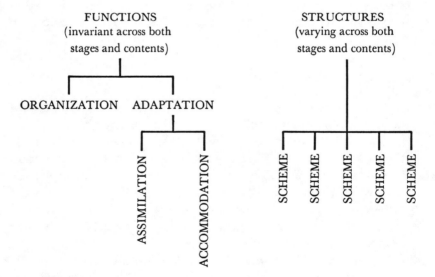

Figure 1.1

RELATIONS AMONG CONCEPTS

Figure 1.1 is an attempt to represent the relationships among *function, organization, adaptation, accommodation, assimilation, structure,* and *scheme.* It will not be a successful attempt, however, if the diagram is conceived as an ordinary classification hierarchy in which, at any given level, each category is a viable entity unto itself. Having divided a deck of cards into spades, hearts, diamonds, and clubs, you can throw away all the hearts, say, or all the clubs, without affecting the contents of the remaining categories; those categories still exist, and in the same form as before. But without *assimilation,* there can be no *accommodation;* and *accommodation* is a change in *structure,* the function of which is to make possible the *assimilation* of some stimulus pattern that is not entirely familiar. Similarly, unless *adaptation* is *organized,* it is not adaptive. Furthermore, the *structures* that in the diagram are separate from *functions* are really *ways of functioning*—the enduring results of organizing adaptation (or adaptive organizing).

This attempt at extensive qualification of the apparently simple relations depicted in Figure 1.1 may be confusing, but it should serve to emphasize one of the salient features of Piaget's theory: its holism. The various entities in the diagram actually represent different aspects of a single entity: a functioning cognitive system.

EQUILIBRATION

One concept that is not represented by the diagram is that of *equilibration.* The word will not be used often in this book, but the idea to which it refers should be kept constantly in mind while studying Piaget's theory in subsequent chapters, for it was the inspiration for the theory in the first place and remains its overarching principle.

Equilibration is a function of every living system. It is a process of attaining equilibrium between external intrusions and the activities of the organism. From a psychological point of view, those activities may be conceived as strategies for maximizing gains of information and minimizing losses.[10] Equilibration is a mechanism of change that operates over an extended period of time in a developing child. To place it in proper perspective, it should be compared to another such mechanism: *learning*.

Behaviorists think of learning as the formation of associations. A response occurs in the presence of a stimulus, and a bond is formed such that henceforth when that stimulus is presented, that response will occur. Often there is an added requirement that the response be followed immediately by a special kind of stimulus called a *reinforcer*.

Although Piaget does not deny that such learning occurs, he has concluded that the fundamental process in learning is not association. He calls association "learning in the narrow sense," and is not much interested in it. What does interest him is a complex that includes maturation and a different kind of learning—a complex that he calls "development."

Possibly the most important difference between Piaget's developmental theory and traditional learning theory is that in addition to the gradual *accretion of functional associations* (isolated simple structures), Piaget's theory recognizes an intermittent *revision of established structures*—a process that entails qualitative as well as quantitative change. The process by which structures are revised is called equilibration.

Equilibration is "coming into equilibrium." In classical physics, there are two kinds of equilibrium: *static* and *dynamic*. A balance scale with equal weights in the two pans is a system in static equilibrium, as indeed is any body at rest. A thermostat is in dynamic equilibrium; so is a homeostatic biological system, a falling body after its acceleration has ceased, or any other system in which an interchange of forces maintains the system in a constant state. In Piaget's theory, equilibrium is dynamic; it is a system of compensating actions that maintain a steady state. That steady state is a condition of the system in which the internal activities of the organism completely compensate for intrusions from without. Because of the importance of states (stages) in his theory, Piaget has often seemed uninterested in mechanisms of transition from one state to another; but the concept of equilibration is concerned with just those transitions.

An example is the acquisition of *conservation of continuous quantity*. The subject is presented with two identical beakers that have been filled to exactly the same level with fruit juice; one is identified as his, the other as the experimenter's. After the child has acknowledged that the amount of juice is the same in each jar, the experimenter pours the contents of one jar into a short, broad container and that of the other into a tall, thin one.

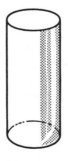

CONTAINER 1   CONTAINER 2

Figure 1.2

"Now," he says to the child, "Do you have more to drink, or do I, or do we have the same amount?" If the answer is "same amount," the subject is said to have "conserved" the substance of the liquid. With respect to this problem, at least, his thinking is "equilibrated."

According to Piaget, this, like all equilibration processes, goes through four steps.[11] In Step 1, the subject attends to only one dimension (usually the height), and he judges the tall drink to be the larger; i.e., he fails to "conserve" quantity. Repeated experiences with configurations that are similar but not identical, however (liquids poured into vessels of varying shapes, from vessel to vessel, etc.), eventually lead him to shift to the other dimension (in this case width). That shift is especially likely when the tall drink is constricted into a mere tube, for then its extreme thinness can hardly escape his attention, and he does indeed state that the tall drink is now the *smaller* of the two. "Focusing on the other dimension" is the second of the four steps of equilibration. The third step is a mixture of the first two—or rather, it is an alternation between them as the conditions of the display are changed. But that alternation, especially if it is rapid, provides the necessary conditions of the fourth step, which is simultaneous attention to both height and width and their coordination into a mutually compensating system. *Now* when he is asked, "Which has more to drink?" he replies firmly "They are the same."

In summary, a child approaches any conservation problem with a strategy for obtaining information from it. But the more consistently he applies that strategy (Step 1), the clearer it becomes to him that it is inadequate; so he shifts to another strategy (Step 2). When the second strategy also fails, he vacillates between the first two (Step 3), which results eventually in a stable system (Step 4) that modifies each and includes both. Now he has information not only about changes in one dimension (e.g., the height of a body of liquid) or about changes in another (e.g., its width), but about both of those plus conservation of whatever remains the same (e.g., the quantity of the liquid) throughout all those changes. The last strategy will not itself disintegrate; but it does contribute to further change, for its very stability makes possible an awareness of inadequacies in larger systems of which it is a part.

Structures continually move toward equilibrium, and when a state of relative equilibrium has been attained, a structure is sharper, more clearly delineated, than it had been previously. But the very sharpness points up inconsistencies and gaps in the structure that had never been salient before. Each equilibrium state therefore carries with it the seeds of its own destruction, for the child's activities are thenceforth directed toward reducing those inconsistencies and closing those gaps. Equilibrium is always dynamic and is never absolute, but the product of each of the major units of development (Sensorimotor, Concrete Operations, and Formal Operations) is a relatively equilibrated system of actions—an *equilibrium.*

FACTORS IN DEVELOPMENT

Equilibration is not the only factor in the intellectual development of a child (though it is the most important). Altogether, there are five:* maturation, physical experience, logico-mathematical experience, social transmission, and equilibration.

MATURATION

To some psychologists, *maturation* is simply [?] the process of attaining maturity, whatever the nature of that process might be. Piaget uses the term more specifically to refer to a gradually unfolding genetic plan. Genetic effects are never seen in isolation, of course; but it does seem worthwhile to abstract them from the flux of life for purposes of analysis. In any case, that is what Piaget has done, and in his writing, "maturation" refers to genetic influences on development.

PHYSICAL EXPERIENCE

Interacting with the genetic effects is a factor called *physical experience,* which the child uses to abstract the various properties of physical objects. Whenever a child squeezes an object and finds it solid, drops it and discovers that it breaks, places it in water and watches it float, or has any other commerce with the object as object, he engages in an abstraction process that results in knowledge of that object and, ultimately, of the material

---

*The categories "physical experience" and "logico-mathematical experience" are often reduced to subcategories under the single category "experience."[12]

of which the object is constituted. The experience is called
physical to distinguish it from logico-mathematical experience,
but paradoxically it always involves assimilation to logico-
mathematical structures. The knowledge that a particular con-
tour is horizontal, for example, depends upon the prior construction of a system of spatial coordinates. "Comparing two
weights presupposes the establishment of a relation, and therefore the construction of a logical form."[13] Even the knowledge
that a single object is "light" or "heavy" entails a comparison
with some internalized standard and, again, presupposes the
construction of a logical form.

LOGICO-MATHEMATICAL EXPERIENCE

It is in the nature of things for a child to act on the objects in his
environment. When he does so, they "act back," so to speak, and
the result is physical experience. But there is another kind of
experience that comes when he constructs *relationships* among
objects—or rather, among his actions on objects. Piaget relates
a story told to him by a mathematician friend who at the age of
four or five years

> . . . was seated on the ground in his garden and he was
> counting pebbles. Now to count these pebbles he put them in
> a row and he counted them one, two, three, up to ten.
> Then he finished counting them and started to count them in
> the other direction. He began by the end and once again he
> found ten. . . . There were ten in one direction and ten in the
> other direction. So he put them in a circle and counted
> them that way and found ten once again.[14]

What that child "learned" (in the broad sense) had to do not
with the physical properties of the pebbles but with the relations
among them. More precisely, what he accomplished was an
organization of his actions with respect to the pebbles.

The concept of "ten"—and the quality of "tenness"— is not a
property of pebbles but a construction of the child's mind. The
experience of that construction, and of others similar to it, is called
logico-mathematical to distinguish it from physical experience.

SOCIAL TRANSMISSSION

The knowledge that a child acquires from physical experience is abstracted from physical objects. In the case of logico-mathematical experience, knowledge is constructed from actions on objects. In social transmission, it comes from other people. They demonstrate, deliberately or otherwise, how things are done; they write things down in books; but mostly they just talk.

And some of their knowledge is acquired by the child. (Which knowledge, and under what conditions it is acquired, we shall discuss in the chapter on educational implications.) Acquisition of knowledge from another person is said to have occurred via *social transmission*.

EQUILIBRATION

Last, but definitely not least, is *equilibration*, which integrates the other four factors into itself. In fact, it is so much a part of them (and they of it) that I personally find it difficult to conceive of equilibration as a factor separate from the others. In any event, its special importance is implicit in the special treatment given to it in the previous section.

DEVELOPMENTAL UNITS

Piaget conceives of intellectual development as a continual process of organization and reorganization of structures, each new organization integrating the previous one into itself. Although that process is continuous, its results are discontinuous; they are qualitatively different from time to time. Because of that, Piaget has chosen to break the total course of development into units called *periods* and *stages*. Note carefully, however, that each of those cross sections of development is described in terms of the *best* the child can do at that time. Many previously acquired behaviors will occur even though he is capable of new and better ones.

TABLE I. UNITS IN THE DEVELOPMENT OF INTELLIGENCE ACCORDING TO PIAGET

Sensorimotor Period—six stages	
Exercising the ready-made sensorimotor schemes	0–1 mo.
Primary circular reactions	1–4 mo.
Secondary circular reactions	4–8 mo.
Coordination of secondary schemes	8–12 mo.
Tertiary circular reactions	12–18 mo.
Invention of new means through mental combinations	18–24 mo.
Preoperational Period	2–7 yr.
Concrete Operations Period	7–11 yr.
Formal Operations Period	11–15 yr.

More refined versions of this table have been devised, and its terms have different meanings in different contexts. The use of the term "stage," for example, is not restricted to the marking off of subunits within the Sensorimotor Period. In the generic sense, it may appear in such expressions as "stage theory" or "moving from one stage of development to another," and it is even used *systematically* in ways that differ from its use in Table I. In one of those uses, the Preoperational Period is called "Stage I"; Concrete Operations, "Stage II"; and Formal Operations, "Stage III." In another, Stage I is early Preoperational, Stage II is late Preoperational, and Stage III is both Concrete and Formal Operational. Thus, even when "stage" is used systematically, that usage may be confined to a particular discussion. In this book, the term will be used only (1) in the generic sense and (2) systematically as in Table I.

There is some justification for classifying "Preoperational" as a subperiod under the Concrete Operations Period. Indeed, that is what was done in the first edition of this book. But current usage is overwhelmingly otherwise, and the newer terms are easier to use. (The term "Preoperational Subperiod of the Concrete Operations Period" is awkward, to say the least; and "Concrete Operational Subperiod of the Concrete Operations Period" is even more so.)

All age ranges are approximations. Among children in any range, one can usually find manifestations of more than one stage or period. The important point is that the *sequence* of development is the same in every child.

Let us now examine the theory in detail, following the outline that appears in Table I. Then, having analyzed each unit in its turn, we'll look back and see whether it is possible to discern the unifying threads that run through all of them.

NOTES

[1] Jean Piaget and Alina Szeminska, *The Child's Conception of Number*, trans. C. Gattengno and F. M. Hodgson (New York: Humanities Press), 1952.

[2] Eleanor Duckworth, "Language and Thought," *in* Milton Schwebel and Jane Raph (eds.), *Piaget in the Classroom* (New York: Basic Books, Inc.), 1973, p. 149.

[3] Robert Rosenthal and K. L. Fade, "The Effect of Experimenter Bias on the Performance of the Albino Rat," *Behavioral Science*, 1963, pp. 183–189, and Robert Rosenthal and R. Lawson, "A Longitudinal Study of Experimenter Bias on the Operant Learning of Laboratory Rats," *Journal of Psychiatric Research*, 1964. An interesting study of the experimenter effect in humans is Robert Rosenthal and Lenore Jacobson, *Pygmalion in the Classroom* (New York: Holt, Rinehart and Winston, Inc.), 1968.

[4] My discussion has been significantly influenced by D. O. Hebb's analysis in his *The Organization of Behavior* (New York: John Wiley & Sons, Inc.), 1949 and in his *A Textbook of Psychology* (Philadelphia: W. B. Saunders), 1958.

[5] Jean Piaget, *The Origins of Intelligence in Children*, trans. Margaret Cook (New York: International Universities Press), 1952, p. 3.

[6] *Ibid.*, p. 8.

[7] *Loc. cit.*

[8] T. G. R. Bower, "The Visual World of Infants," *Scientific American*, vol. 215, no. 6 (December 1966), pp. 80–92, and his "Phenomenal Identity and Form Perception in an Infant," *Journal of Perception and Psychophysics*, 1967, pp. 74–76.

[9] Jean Piaget, "Genetic Epistemology," *Columbia Forum*, Fall, 1969, p. 5.

[10] David Elkind (ed.), *Six Psychological Studies* (New York: Random House, Inc.), 1967, p. 109.

[11] Adapted from John H. Flavell's account in his *The Developmental Psychology of Jean Piaget* (Princeton: D. Van Nostrand Co., Inc.), 1963, pp. 215–249.

[12] Jean Piaget and Bärbel Inhelder, *The Psychology of the Child*, trans. Helen Weaver (New York: Basic Books), 1969, pp. 155–156.

[13] *Ibid.*, p. 155.

[14] Jean Piaget, "Development and Learning," *in* R. E. Ripple and V. N. Rockcastle (eds.), *Piaget Rediscovered* (Ithaca: Cornell Univ. Press), 1964. [Originally published as a section of *Journal of Research in Science Teaching*, vol. 2, 1964, p. 179.]

2

Sensorimotor Period (0-2 years)

2

Sensorimotor Period

Cognitive development probably begins before birth, but since Piaget's observations start at that point, that is where we shall begin. To those who are preparing for some kind of work in public education, even that may seem too early; but remember that our objective is to understand intellectual development. Given that objective, the earliest adaptations must be recognized as fundamental. Later developments are built upon foundations laid in infancy.

The organization of behavior has its roots in genetic programming and the repetitive patterning of inputs. The most primitive subsystems (the reflexes) are almost entirely preempted by the genes, but even they accommodate to the inputs that evolution has designed them to assimilate, and most of them become available for organization into systems that have *not* been predetermined in any precise way. They become the interacting elements of new, more elaborate structures, or schemes. It takes many repetitions to form each of those elemental schemes; but once they are established, a new super-scheme may be formed in an instant. Cognitive changes in an adult, then, are *different* from those in an infant—not only because of the maturation of his nervous system, but also because of the interactions that he has had with his environment.

Piaget has conceived a more comprehensive interpretation of the period of infancy than have most workers in the field. Few of them have dealt with infancy as a period of intellectual growth at all. But Piaget shows how the necessary processes of symbolic intelligence begin developing at birth and how a shift occurs later from motor symbols to conceptual symbols. Some theorists have seen adult intelligence as an elaboration of motor symbols; others have dealt only with conceptual symbols. Piaget has shown that one grows out of the other.

THE SIX STAGES

Probably no other feature of Piaget's system has been opposed with so much vigor as his conception of *stages*. "There are so many influences on a child's development," say the critics, "how could they possibly combine to produce the same 'stage' of development in every child of a given age?"

Piaget has not given a completely satisfactory answer to those critics. Nevertheless, the concept of stage can be useful if we keep in mind three things: (1) that different children may pass through the sequence of stages at different rates, (2) that each stage is named for the process that has most recently become operative, even though others may occur at the same time in their original form and (3) that each stage is marked by the formation of a total structure that includes its predecessors within it as necessary substructures.

Notice that in Figure 2.1 the period within the brackets is labeled "Stage *B*," even though Process *A* is in full operation and Process *C* has begun to develop. For a "gifted" child, all these curves would be steeper, closer together, and shifted to the left (the processes develop faster), and for a "retarded" child, they would be flatter, farther apart, and shifted to the right (the processes develop more slowly). For each child, however, Piaget

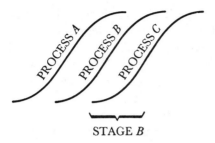

STAGE *B*

Figure 2.1

maintains that the *sequence* remains the same. And finally, *B* includes *A*, and *C* includes both *A* and *B*; the overall structure that characterizes any given stage is an integration of those that preceded it, and the achievements of that stage are preparations for those of the next.

STAGE 1 (0–1 MONTH). EXERCISING THE READY-MADE SENSORIMOTOR SCHEMES

The infant is born with a number of sensorimotor mechanisms "wired in." (A familiar term for them is "reflexes.") He makes orienting responses to light or sound; his hand grasps an object placed in his palm; he sucks when his lips are touched; he vocalizes, waves his arms, etc., in response to any strong stimulus. That is not a complete list of innate mechanisms; the list need not be extended here, however, for Piaget is interested not so much in hereditary organizations *per se* as in the alterations that occur in them as the child interacts with his environment.

The first stage, therefore, may be passed over lightly. Keep in mind, however, that organized patterns of activity are being formed during this period that will enter into, and in fact be basic to the development of, more complex functioning later on.

STAGE 2 (1–4 MONTHS). PRIMARY CIRCULAR REACTIONS

Primary Circular Reactions are called "primary" because they are centered on the infant's body rather than on external objects and "circular" because they are endlessly repeated. The child stumbles onto an act that produces a new experience and then repeats the act to reproduce the experience. This stage is marked by (1) variations in the schemes as more and more stimulus patterns are assimilated, (2) coordination of various schemes as functional relationships are developed among them—e.g., hearing and looking at the same object, seeing and reaching-grasping the same object, reaching-grasping and sucking the same object—and (3) perceptual recognition of objects as a result of repeated stimulation.

Piaget's observations indicate that knowing is an active, building process. For example, "just looking" becomes "looking in order to see," as indicated by the infant's differential responses to various objects. Originally, he reacts to all objects indiscriminately; later, he looks more at some than others, smiles at some more than others, etc. Reaching and touching is repeated many times with apparent pleasure. Sucking is continued on some objects, discontinued on others.

During this period, the behavior of the child begins to be centered on *objects*; but to him there is no objective reality—no general space or time, no permanence of objects. There are only *events*—i.e., components of the child's own functioning. When an object in his field of vision disappears, it ceases to exist. Without permanence of objects, there can be no general space (though there are the beginnings of visual space, auditory space, tactual space, etc.). *Time* is similarly limited to that which encompasses a single event, such as moving a hand from leg to face, feeling the nipple and beginning to suck, or hearing a sound and seeing its source.

Overt activity is necessary to the development that occurs in this stage. Piaget noted that one of his children was retarded in "hand-watching" coordination. The child had been born in the winter, and to give her as much sun as possible it was necessary to take her outside bundled in blankets. Thus she was prevented from engaging in the activity from which hand-watching develops.

To summarize: during the second stage there is progress toward integration of the biologically given patterns of the infant into habits and perceptions. The reflexes of Stage 1 were pure assimilation, but these changes are the reciprocal effects of assimilation and accommodation.

STAGE 3 (4–8 MONTHS). SECONDARY CIRCULAR REACTIONS

The stage of secondary circular reactions is so called because the center of interest is not the body's actions but the environmental consequences of those actions (hence the term "secondary") and because they are repetitive and self-reinforcing* (which makes them "circular"). A useful prototype might be "shaking a rattle to hear the noise." The reaching-and-grasping is done in anticipation of the listening-to-the-noise, and the two have been amalgamated into a new unit: a *circular reaction*.

Intention and Means-End Relations

Many of Piaget's interpretive comments have been deleted from the following quotation. Can you identify the behaviors from which he infers "intention"?

> *Observation 94:*
> [At three months, five days] Lucienne shakes her bassinet by moving her legs violently (bending and unbending them, etc.), which makes the cloth dolls swing from the hood. Lucienne looks at them smiling, and recommences at once. . . . The next day, I present the dolls: Lucienne immediately moves, shakes her legs, but this time without smiling. . . . At age three months, eight days, I find Lucienne swinging her dolls. An hour later I make them move slightly: Lucienne looks at them, smiles, stirs a little, then resumes looking at her hand as she was doing shortly before. A chance movement disturbs the dolls: Lucienne again looks at them and this time shakes herself with regularity. She stares at the dolls, barely smiles, and moves her legs vigorously and thoroughly. . . .

---

*As used here, the term "reinforcement" is intended to imply only an empirical relationship, not a hypothetical construct. The empirical fact is that the child does repeat the activity without being exposed to any "reinforcing stimulus" that is external to it.

At three months, thirteen days, Lucienne looks at her hand with more coordination than usual. In her joy at seeing her hand come and go between her face and the pillow, she shakes herself in front of this hand as when faced by the dolls. Now this reaction of the shaking appears to remind her of the dolls, which she looks at immediately, as though she foresaw their movement. . . . At age three months, sixteen days, as soon as I suspend the dolls she immediately shakes them, without smiling, with precise and rhythmical movements with quite an interval between shakes. . . . At four months, four days, in a new bassinet, she moves her loins violently in order to shake the hood. At four months, thirteen days, she moves her legs very rapidly while looking at the festoons on the bassinet hood: as soon as she sees them again, after a pause, she begins once more. . . .

At four months, twenty-seven days, Lucienne is lying in her bassinet. I hand a doll from the hood over her feet. This immediately sets in motion the schema of shaking. Her feet reach the doll and give it a violent movement, which Lucienne surveys with delight. Afterward she looks at her motionless foot for a second, then recommences. . . .

At five months, eighteen days, I place the doll at different heights, sometimes to the left, sometimes to the right: Lucienne tries to reach it with her foot, and then, when she has succeeded, she shakes it. . . .[1]

Before he will say that an act is *intentional*, Piaget requires that it show three characteristics:

1. Object-centered orientation.
2. Intermediate acts (means) preceding the goal act (end).
3. Deliberate adaptation to a new situation.

It is clear from Observation 94 that Lucienne's behavior meets the first two of these requirements. As for the third, Piaget does not give us an operational definition of "deliberate" adaptation, but he apparently infers it from the often serious visage, the pause between presentation of the stimulus and initiation of the response, and the constant end effect—in this example, the swinging of the dolls.

But the schemes underlying this behavior are only the beginnings of "intention and means-ends separation," because in them the relation of means to end is fortuitous. The infant apparently comes to anticipate an interesting spectacle whenever he produces a certain action; but does this really meet the criterion of "deliberateness"? Later on, the action and the effect will be clearly differentiated, and both will be subsumed under a strong intentional scheme. The difference is one of degree, but it is a difference; intention and means-end separation do *not* appear full-blown in Stage 3.

Motor Meaning

Here is another series of observations, again with most of the interpretations deleted. The inference in this example will probably be a little more difficult to grasp than the preceding one. See if you can tease it out.

> *Observation 107:*
> At age five months, three days, Lucienne tries to grasp a spool suspended above her by means of elastic bands. . . . She manages to touch but not to grasp them. Having shaken them fortuitously, she then breaks off to shake herself for a moment while looking at them, but then she resumes her attempts at grasping. . . . Why has she broken off in order to shake herself for a few seconds? It was not in order to shake the spool, because she did not persevere and because she was busy with something else at the moment; neither was it in order to facilitate her attempts at grasping. . . .
> At age five months, ten days, Lucienne again relapses into states identical to those with the dolls. At age six months, five days, she shakes herself several times in succession. It is *an outline of some action suggested by this sight.* . . . [Italics added.]
> At six months, twelve days, Lucienne perceives from a distance two celluloid parrots attached to a chandelier. These she had sometimes had on the hood of her bassinet. As soon as she sees them, she definitely but briefly shakes her legs, but without trying to act upon them from a distance.
> . . . At six months, nineteen days, it suffices that she catches sight of her dolls from a distance (these are dolls that she had previously learned to swing with her hands) for her to outline the movement of swinging them with her hand. .
> From seven months, twenty-seven days, certain highly familiar situations no longer set in motion secondary

circular reactions, but simply outlines of the schemata. Thus when seeing a doll that she actually had swung many times, Lucienne limits herself to opening and closing her hands or shaking her legs, but very briefly and without real effort. . . . *It is only a sort of acknowledgment.*[2] [Italics added.]

Note especially (1) the increasing *brevity* of the motor response as the pattern develops and (2) the apparent *lack of intention*; the action appears instead to be *representing* the object. I submit that the responses that the child has made to an object are, in effect, its *meaning*. For you and me, the meaning of an object or event consists entirely of implicit motor responses and other mediating processes. In the child, those responses become increasingly covert as he grows older; but at this stage his central processes are not yet sufficiently elaborated or organized for meaning to be "mental." It is rather, as Piaget puts it, "an outline of some action . . ."*

Incorporation of New Objects into Existing Schemes

Related to this "outline of action" is the behavior described in the following brief excerpt:

Observation 110:
[At three months, twenty-nine days] Laurent sees for the first time the paper knife. He grasps and looks at it, but only for a moment. Afterward he immediately swings it with his right hand as he does all objects grasped. He then rubs it by chance against the wicker of the bassinet and tries to produce the sound heard as though the knife were the rattle he has used for this purpose. It then suffices that I place the object in his left hand for him to shake it in the same fashion. . . .[5]

---

*"Motor meaning" (the term used as the heading for this section) is my own term, not Piaget's. He speaks of "motor recognition" and of "recognitory assimilation"; but the initial referent of each of these is the very first differentiation of responses in Stage 1[3]—i.e., the barest beginning of the differential (to various objects) responses that become clearly observable later, in Stage 2.[4] Motor meaning is more complex, and does not appear until Stage 3.

Piaget refers to the knife as an *aliment* for habitual schemes. By swinging objects, shaking them, and rubbing them against the side of the crib, new objects are assimilated into existing schemes.

Object Permanence and the Construction of Space

You and I are wont to assume that the real world is there, that we apprehend it as it is (assuming that there is nothing wrong with our sensory apparatus), and that's all there is to it! Actually, however, some of the most rudimentary perceptions are achieved only after a great deal of experience. (See Chapter 1, pp. 10–11.)

The inference that an object has a *permanence* beyond our immediate perception of it comes about even more slowly; it does not even begin in the average child until the stage being discussed now.* We know that it does begin at this stage because of a particular change in his behavior in a certain kind of situation —namely, one in which he has been attending to an object and it is suddenly removed from his visual field. Before, he would simply shift his attention to something else; now he may search for the absent object.

Children in Stage 3 do in fact engage in some searching for absent objects, but at this age it is of very brief duration, and it is confined to one modality—e.g., a felt object will be groped for but not looked for, and a seen object will be looked for but not groped for.

Related to the permanence of objects is the development of space and time dimensions. Whereas space had previously been confined to that mediated by a single modality, or even locality, of input (e.g., visual, tactile-kinesthetic, or buccal), in the third stage these various spaces become organized into what Piaget calls a *grouping*.

---

*Psychiatrists have coined the term, "separation anxiety" to refer to the distress that is occasioned by the absence of the mother. But how can the child be distressed about being separated from her if she does not exist when she is not present? The answer is, he can't; and in point of fact, separation anxiety does not occur in Stages 1 or 2. Its development is correlated, as one might suspect, with that of object permanence; until then, it is literally a case of "out of sight, out of mind."

This grouping comes about as a result of the infant's increasing coordination of seeing, reaching-grasping, and sucking. As the child becomes more adept at these coordinations, he begins to move objects about, and eventually his interest expands to include relations among objects, as opposed to an exclusive concern with relations of objects to his actions with respect to them. This expansion is the beginning (but only the beginning) of a conception of *general space*.

STAGE 4 (8–12 MONTHS). COORDINATION OF SECONDARY SCHEMES

The title of the fourth stage is not very descriptive. Suffice it to say that in this stage there are refinements in each of the four categories that were used in analyzing Stage 3 (i.e., *Intention and Means-End Separation, Meaning, Incorporation of New Objects into Existing Schemes* and *Object Permanence and the Construction of Space*). Beyond those, we shall need a new category of *Causality*.

Intention and Means-End Relations

Here is another set of observations from *The Origins of Intelligence*. See what you make of it:

> [When he is six months of age] I present Laurent with a match box, extending my other hand laterally to make an obstacle to his prehension. Laurent tries to pass over my hand or to the side, but he does not attempt to displace it. . . .
> Same reactions at age six months, eight days; six months, ten days; six months, twenty-one days; . . . and seven months, ten days. . . .
> Finally, at seven months, thirteen days, Laurent reacts quite differently. I present a box above my obstacle hand, but behind it, so that he cannot reach the matches without setting the obstacle aside. After trying to take no notice of it, Laurent suddenly hits my obstacle hand as though to remove or lower it. I let him [lower the hand], and he grasps the box. I recommence to bar his passage, but I use as a screen a sufficiently supple cushion to keep the impress of the child's gestures. Laurent tries to reach the box, and, bothered by the

obstacle, he at once strikes it, definitely lowering it until the way is clear.

With Laurent seven months and seventeen days old, I resume the experiment without there having been intervening attempts. First I present the object (my watch) 10 cm. behind the cushion (the object of course being visible). Laurent tries at first to grasp the watch, then pauses to hit the cushion. . . . With Laurent age seven months twenty-eight days, instead of simply hitting the things that intercede between his hand and the object, Laurent applies himself to pushing them away or even to displacing them. . . . I present him a little bell 5 cm. behind the cushion. Laurent first strikes the cushion, as previously, but then depresses it with one hand while he grasps the object with the other. Same reaction with my hand. At age seven months, twenty-nine days, he immediately depresses the cushion with his left hand in order to reach the match box with his right. At eight months, one day, when my hand intervenes with the obstacle, I definitely feel that he depresses it and pushes harder and harder to overcome my resistance. . . . At nine months, fifteen days, he pushes my hand away with his left hand while pulling at the object with his right. . . .[6]

No doubt the clearest impression that you received from these observations was that of *intention*—Laurent's dogged determination to reach the object despite the interposition of barriers to his actions.

But in the process of attaining his goal, he made use of a cleanly articulated subaction—that of removing the barrier. That sub-action represents a further development of the separation of *means* from *ends*. In fact, it is at this stage that the first unequivocal manifestation of that separation can be observed. The infant in the third stage had produced certain effects by responding in certain ways, like making things move by shaking the crib or by pushing the object. But that was only the beginning of intention and means-end separation. There, he lost interest if an obstacle were interposed between him and an object. In this stage, he attacks the obstacle. From these observations, it is clear that there is now a relatively clear separation of means from ends, and intention is a most compelling inference.

As will be shown later, the separation of means from ends has far-reaching implications. When the two are completely separated and the end drops out (the means becomes an end in itself), we have *play*; when they are differentiated but continually related, we have *problem-solving* behavior. Both originate in this primitive separation of means from ends.

Symbolic Meaning

You will recall that in Stage 3 the infant acknowledged the presence of an object by reinstating some bit of overt behavior that had previously occurred in its presence. Now, in Stage 4, something new has been added:

> *Observation 133:*
> At age nine months, sixteen days, Jacqueline . . . likes the grape juice in a glass, but not the soup in a bowl. She watches her mother's activity. When the spoon comes out of the glass she opens her mouth wide, whereas when the spoon comes from the bowl, her mouth remains closed. Her mother tries to lead her to make a mistake by taking a spoon from the bowl and passing it by the glass before offering it to Jacqueline. But she is not fooled. . . . At age nine months, eighteen days, Jacqueline no longer needs to look at the spoon. She notes by the sound whether the spoonful comes from the glass or the bowl and obstinately closes her mouth [when it comes from the bowl]. . . .[7]

Another example of the same phenomenon occurred when, at eleven months and fifteen days, Jacqueline cried whenever her mother put on a hat.

When in Stage 3 the child recognized an object by reproducing an action that had previously occurred in its presence, I spoke of that action as the "meaning" of the object. In Stage 4, the "actions" consist primarily of complex neural patterns that serve to "represent" the object, and the overt responses are not to the sensory input itself (the glass, the bowl, the hat) but to its "symbolic meaning" (grape juice, soup, mother's departure).

Thus in place of the "motor meaning" of Stage 3, we have a "symbolic meaning" in Stage 4.

Incorporation of New Objects into Existing Schemes

Actions summarized by this title are so obvious that the category is included here mainly for reasons of symmetry—i.e., so that the discussion will parallel that of Stage 3. It is the nature of cognitive structures to apply themselves repeatedly to whatever parts of the environment can be assimilated by them, and that process continues through the waking hours of every normal person on every day of his life.

Object Permanence and the Construction of Space

As already noted, the "reality" that surrounds us is a construction of the brain; moreover, the ability to make that construction is not given but acquired.

The following observation illustrates one of those acquisitions as it functions in Stage 4:

> *Observation 44:*
> [At nine months, seventeen days] Laurent is placed on a sofa between a coverlet (*A*) on the right and a wool garment (*B*) on the left. I place my watch under *A*; he gently raises the coverlet, perceives part of the object, uncovers it, and grasps it. The same thing happens a second and a third time. . . . I then place the watch under *B*; Laurent watches this maneuver attentively, but at the moment the watch has disappeared under *B*, he turns back toward *A* and searches for the object under that screen. I again place the watch under *B*; he again searches for it under *A*. . . .[8]

It is very interesting to note the similarity between this behavior and that of the famous McGill scotties. These animals had been raised to adulthood in small cubicles that deprived them of the varied experiences that normal dogs have while they are growing up; they had never even seen their keeper. Of the many tests administered to the dogs when they were removed from the cubicle,[9] the one depicted in Figure 2.2 seems especially similar to the Piaget "experiment" just quoted.

In the McGill experiment, a piece of food was placed at *A*, and the dog was carried to within a few inches of the food so as to be certain that he was attending to it. Then, with the dog

Figure 2.2

watching from *C*, where he was being restrained by the experimenter, the food was moved to *B*. When the dog was released, he did not approach the place (*B*) to which the food had been moved, but trotted directly to the place (*A*) where he had originally seen it.

Don't the McGill experiment and Piaget's Observation 44 appear to be the same test with the same result? From a commonsense point of view, it is certainly an unexpected result; but from Piaget's point of view, it is just what should be expected. Later structures are built upon a foundation of earlier ones. In this, Piaget's fourth stage of the Sensorimotor Period, there is a shift in the child's conceptualization from object reality dependent on his own actions to object reality dependent on the surround.

The result is a kind of "context-bound object permanence." Or perhaps a more fitting inference—though it is not made explicitly by Piaget—is that this behavior represents instead an "overpermanence" of the object: it is still there to the child, even after it has been moved away. It is as though the central process representing the object is tied securely to others representing its immediate surround.* To put it another way, he

---

*Even though I speak here of central processes that "represent" the object and its surround, Piaget does not acknowledge "true representation" until "no perceived sign commands belief in permanency." In this example, the screen is the "sign of the actual presence of the object"; thus we are not dealing here with a true representation.[11]

sees "the object-I-find-at-*A*" being hidden, and he fails to assimilate the object in its new hiding place.[10]

The perception of space continues to develop during this period. Briefly, what happens is that the child becomes interested in objects as objects rather than as mere aliments to his motor schemes. Whereas new objects previously had arrested his attention only briefly before he did something with them, now he examines each object carefully in every possible way, as though it presents a problem to him.

One result is that the child gains the ability to reverse an object. For example, earlier, when handed a bottle backward, the infant would make no effort to turn it around; now, he immediately reverses it so that the nipple is toward him. It will be a long time before he can recognize what an object looks like from a different point of view, but this does seem to be a step in that direction.

Causality

It is in this fourth stage that we see for the first time clear indications of a construction that is anything like what an adult means by *causality*.

Previously, the infant was involved initially in every transaction that made any impression upon him; now, he can perceive objects other than himself as causes. The evidence for this is that he attacks barriers (as if they were "causing" his frustration) and that he sometimes waits for adults to do things for him (again indicating that there is a "cause" outside himself). There is a shift of interest from the action to its effect.

STAGE 5 (12–18 MONTHS). TERTIARY CIRCULAR REACTIONS

The Secondary Circular Reaction of Stage 3 was a consolidation of certain motor schemes by repetition of activities that produce "interesting spectacles" that are integral parts of the activities themselves but that reinforce those activities. The Tertiary Circular Reaction of Stage 5 is essentially the same process on a higher level: the "spectacle" is now separate from the overt action. The reaction is called "tertiary" because instead of being concerned with actions of his own body, as in Primary Circular Reactions, or predominantly with the direct environmental consequences of those simple acts, as in Secondary Circular Reactions, the child now engages in "experiments" in order to discover new properties of objects and events.

Intention and Means-End Separation

Here is a series of examples that illustrate the transition from secondary to tertiary reactions:

> *Observation 141:*
> This first example will make us understand the transition between secondary and "tertiary" reactions: that of the well-known behavior pattern by means of which the child explores distant space and constructs his representation of movement: the behavior pattern of letting go of objects or of throwing them in order subsequently to pick them up.
>
> One recalls (Obs. 140) how [at ten months, five days] Laurent discovered in "exploring" a case of soap, the possibility of throwing this object and letting it fall. What interested him at first was not the objective phenomenon of the fall, but the very act of letting go. He observed fortuitously, which still constitutes a "secondary" reaction, "derived," it is true, but of typical structure.
>
> [At ten months, ten days, however] the reaction changes and becomes "tertiary." That day Laurent manipulates a small piece of bread (without any alimentary interest: he has never eaten any and has no thought of tasting it) and lets it go continually. He even breaks off fragments, which he lets drop. Now, in contradistinction to what has happened on the preceding days, *he pays no attention to the act of letting go*, whereas *he watches with great interest the body in motion*; in particular he looks at it for a long time when it has fallen, and picks it up when he can. [Italics added.]
>
> [At ten months, eleven days] Laurent is lying on his back but nevertheless resumes his experiments of the day before. He grasps in succession a celluloid swan, and box, etc., stretches out his arm and lets them fall. He distinctly varies the positions of the fall. Sometimes he stretches out his arm vertically, sometimes he holds it obliquely, in front of or behind his eyes, etc. When the object falls in a new position

(for example, on his pillow), he lets it fall two or three times more on the same place, as though to study the spatial relation; then he modifies the situation. At a certain moment the swan falls near his mouth; now, he does not suck it (even though this object habitually serves this purpose), but drops it three times more while merely making the gesture of opening his mouth.

Observation 146:
[At one year, two months, eight days] Jacqueline holds in her hands an object which is new to her; a round, flat box, which she turns all over, shakes, rubs against the bassinet, etc. She lets it go and tries to pick it up. But she only succeeds in touching it with her index finger, without grasping it. She nevertheless makes an attempt and presses on the edge. The box then tilts up and falls again. Jacqueline, very much interested in this fortuitous result, immediately applies herself to studying it. Hitherto it is only a question of an attempt at assimilation analogous to that of Observations 136 and 137, and of the fortuitous discovery of a new result, but this discovery, *instead of giving rise to a simple circular reaction, is at once extended to "experiments in order to see."* [Italics added.]

In effect, Jacqueline immediately rests the box on the ground and pushes it as far as possible (it is noteworthy that care is taken to push the box far away in order to reproduce the same conditions as in the first attempt, as though this were a necessary condition for obtaining the result). Afterward Jacqueline puts her finger on the box and presses it. But as she places her finger on the center of the box she simply displaces it and makes it slide instead of tilting it up. She amuses herself with this game and keeps it up (resumes it after intervals, etc.) for several minutes. Then, changing the point of contact, she finally again places her finger on the edge of the box, which tilts it up. She repeats this many times, varying the conditions, but keeping track of her discovery: now she only presses on the edge![12]

How do these adaptations differ from earlier ones? Doesn't the child indeed appear to be "experimenting" with new combinations of responses? And did you notice the continued slight variations as the pattern was repeated?

The "repetition of activities that produce interesting spectacles" is at a higher level here than in Stage 3, because instead of merely activating the pattern in a stereotyped manner, this child deliberately manipulates the environment to find out what happens, and continues to vary his approach even after an "interesting spectacle" has occurred. One is tempted to think of the Stage 5 baby as "the first scientist"!

Object Permanence, Space, and Time

Although the following quotation is very short, you may find in it evidence of advances in all three of the title categories. Try it and see.

> *Observation 54:*
> [At eleven months, twenty-two days] Laurent is seated between two cushions, *A* and *B*. I hide my watch alternately under each: Laurent constantly searches for the object where it has just disappeared—that is, sometimes under *A*, and sometimes under *B*, without remaining attached to the first, privileged position as during the fourth stage. . . .[13]

Isn't it a reasonable inference that the object is now being represented by an internal symbol? And did you notice the new independence of the object from its surround?

This new level of *object permanence* is a function of the subject's altered perception of space; and notice that a temporal sequence is also involved. There is internal representation of the object, and that representation has a unity and an independence not previously achieved. *Object permanence*—or the negation of "overpermanence" (p. 38)—and *space perception* and *time perception* are all revealed at a higher level here than in the previous stage.

Subsequent observations indicate a limitation, however: these sequential displacements of an object can be followed only if the displacements are visible. If a toy is placed inside an open box and then the box is placed behind a screen and emptied there, the child will not think to look behind the screen for the toy when the empty box is handed to him.

Causality

The child's conception of *causality* also has been further developed. He engages in some true imitation at this stage, and that has some implications for causality; but since I wish to treat imitation longitudinally after examining the other developments in the Sensorimotor Period, I shall not discuss it here.

Recall that in Stage 4 the child showed some appreciation of external causes by waiting for adults to serve him. Now, he not only waits, but actively solicits their help—to reach, push, open, etc.

The elaboration of means also has causative significance. When the child learns to use a stick or a string—e.g., to pull something toward him—he is constrained to *discriminate* between himself and the tool as the immediate cause of the movement of the object. This represents another step away from his original "the-world-is-my-actions-upon-it" conception of reality. His manipulation of objects begins at a higher level in this stage because of the means-end differentiation that has occurred in the previous one. In Stage 5 his behavior becomes even more purposive, as he continues to differentiate a variety of ends, and especially a variety of means.

The necessary culmination of this proliferation of means to a given end is a counter-trend in which ineffective means are discarded. Here is an example.

> *Observation 162:*
> [At fifteen months, twelve days] Jacqueline is seated in her playpen whose four sides are formed by vertical bars connected at base and summit by horizontal bars. The bars are 6 cm apart. Outside the pen, parallel to the sides where Jacqueline is, I place a stick 20 cm long, which takes up the distance of about three spaces between the bars. We shall call these spaces, *a*, *b*, and *c*; space *b* corresponds to the middle part of the stick, and spaces *a* and *c* to the end parts. The problem is to transfer this stick from outside to inside the pen.
>
> (1) Jacqueline begins by grasping the stick through space *b*. She raises it along the bars but holds it horizontally and parallel to the frame so that the harder she pulls the less it moves. She then extends her other hand through *c*, but holds the stick horizontally and does not succeed in making it come through. She finally lets go of the object which I put back in its initial position.

(2) Jacqueline begins over again by grasping the stick at *c*. In raising it, she tilts it up a little, by chance, and so makes it slightly oblique. She immediately takes advantage of what she perceives and, passing her hand through *c*, she tilts the stick until it is sufficiently vertical to pass through. She then brings it into the playpen through *b*. Why did she tilt it up? Was it through foresight or did she simply extend the movement, which was due to chance, so as to see what would happen?

(3–4) This time Jacqueline grasps the stick through space *c* at one of its ends. She draws it horizontally against the bars, but encountering resistance from them, she quickly makes it vertical and passes it through without difficulty. The speed of this adaptation is due to the fact that the stick was grasped by one of its ends.

(5) Jacqueline grasps the stick by the middle, at *b*. She raises it, puts it horizontally against the bars as in (1). She pulls and seems very surprised by a failure. It is only after a while that she tilts it and succeeds in bringing it in.

(6–10) Same reactions. At each new attempt, she begins by trying to make it penetrate horizontally parallel to the frame. Only after this initial failure does she tilt up the stick, still quite slowly.

(11) This time Jacqueline turns the stick more rapidly because she grasps it at *c*.

(12–15) She again grasps it at *b* and recommences to try to bring it through horizontally. Then she tilts it up, more slowly than at (11), and succeeds.

(16) She continues to take it at *b* and to try to pull it through horizontally, but this time she does not persist and tilts it up immediately.

(17) For the first time Jacqueline tilts the stick before it has touched the bar, and no longer tries to bring it in horizontally even though she grasped it at the middle.

(18–19) She begins by trying to bring it through horizontally, but it seems that this was due to automatism and she tilts it up immediately afterward.

(20 *et seq.*) She finally turns it systematically before it touches the bars.[14]

Surely—but very slowly—the ineffective means drop out, until eventually the performance becomes deliberate and efficient. The process by which it becomes so certainly appears to be what Thorndike called "trial-and-error" and what Skinner might refer to as the selection of one response by "reinforcement."* Piaget prefers "groping accommodation," because he says that the errors are not random responses, but rather that they are *inappropriate generalizations* of schemes that have been effective in other situations; the new situation is assimilated to the old scheme (reach-grasp-pull) without adequate accommodation of that scheme to the new situation (the bars).† In any case, it is clear that in Stage 5 there has been a shift from stereotyped behavior to a kind of systematic variation of responses.

---

*Others have referred to it as "hypothesis testing," but the term "hypothesis," though not anathema to Piaget, as is "reinforcement," is not one that he would use. Piaget does not recognize "hypotheses" until the Period of Formal Operations.

†When he repeated the bars problem with other objects (a book, a doll, a cardboard rooster), Piaget found, just as Harlow did later in his "learning-how-to-learn" experiments with monkeys, that his subject had to learn each solution from the beginning (in this case by pulling the object against the bars) but that, also like Harlow's monkeys, she learned each solution more quickly than the previous one. Two other pertinent studies of nonhuman primates are those of Köhler and Birch (see Bibliography). Köhler had found very little of this "trial-and-error" in his chimpanzee subjects; but other psychologists later found that for subjects of the same species, working on the same problem that Köhler had given to his subjects (using a stick as an extension of the arm to rake in a distant piece of food), trial and error was the rule rather than the exception. Birch suspected that the critical difference might be related to the fact that his subjects were reared in the laboratory, whereas Köhler's animals had grown up in the jungle. He therefore arranged for several of his "failures" to have free-play experiences with sticks, then retested them afterwards. Every one of them solved the problem almost immediately, even though the sticks had not been used as rakes during the free-play period. Piaget would probably say that Birch's animals developed an extension-of-the-arm scheme during the free-play situation and that it (the extension-of-the-arm scheme) was later reciprocally assimilated to an already established reach-grasp-pull scheme to solve the problem.

STAGE 6 (18–24 MONTHS). INVENTION OF NEW MEANS
THROUGH MENTAL COMBINATION

The sixth and last stage of the Sensorimotor Period is, it seems to me, actually a transitional phase—transitional to the subsequent stage, the Preoperational Period. But I suppose that is what one should expect, since every unit in the series is transitional to the next.

Intention and Means-End Relations

The sixth stage is virtually defined by the important change that occurs in this category, Intention and Means-End Relations. It concerns the invention of new means through mental combinations. If one examines the entire Sensorimotor Period, one can discern four forms of intentionality and goal-directed behavior:

1) Applying familiar schemes to familiar situations (Stage 3).
2) Applying familiar schemes to new situations (Stage 4).
3) Modifying familiar schemes to fit new situations (Stage 5).
4) Invention of new means through reciprocal assimilation of schemes (Stage 6).

The behavior of a child in this sixth stage is more like that of Köhler's jungle-reared chimps than that of Birch's laboratory-reared animals.* If you will recall my interpretation of the differences between the initial behavior patterns of those two groups of chimpanzees in the stick problem (Köhler's jungle-reared animals had had a richer "early experience" than Birch's), I think it will be relatively easy to interpret the differences Piaget reports between the way in which Laurent, on the one hand, and his sisters, on the other, acquired what Piaget calls "the pattern of the stick." The account is rather a long one, but its length is the very point of the illustration. See if you can tell why.

---

*What was tangential to the discussion on pages 43–45 is now central; read the footnote on p. 45 again with the present context in mind.

Observation 177:
In contrast to Jacqueline and Lucienne, who were submitted
to numerous experiments during which they had opportunity
to "learn" to use the stick, Laurent only manipulated it at
long intervals until such time as he knew how to use it
spontaneously. In order to characterize that moment, it is
worthwhile to retrace briefly the ensemble of Laurent's
earlier behavior patterns relating to the stick.

As early as four months and twenty days of age, i.e., at
the beginning of the third stage, Laurent is confronted by a
short stick, which he assimilates by shaking it, rubbing it
against the wicker of his bassinet, etc. In general, he makes it
the equivalent of the paper knife. . . . At four months and
twenty-one days, when Laurent is holding the stick, he
happens to strike a hanging toy and immediately continues.

But during the next hours, Laurent no longer tries to
reproduce this result even when I put the stick back in his
hand. This is not, then, an example of "the behavior pattern
of the stick." . . . The following days I give him the stick
again and try to make him associate it to the activity of the
various schemata, but Laurent does not react then or in the
following weeks. . . . In the course of the fourth stage,
characterized by the coordination of the schemata, he makes
no progress in the use of the stick. During this stage, however,
Laurent comes to use the hand of another person as an intermediate to act upon distant objects, thus succeeding in
spatializing causality and preparing the way for experimental
behavior. But when, at eight months or even nine months,
I give Laurent the stick, he only uses it to strike around him
and not to displace or to bring to him the objects he hits. . . .

[At twelve months], i.e., well into the fifth stage, when
Jacqueline and Lucienne succeeded in "discovering" the
utilization of the stick, Laurent manipulates a long wooden
ruler for a long time, but arrives at only the three following
reactions: (1) turning the stick over systematically while
transferring it from one hand to the other, (2) striking the
floor, his shoes and various objects with it, (3) displacing it by
pushing it gently over the floor with his index finger. Several
times I place at certain distances from Laurent some attractive
object to see whether he, already holding the stick, will know
how to use it. Each time, Laurent tries to attain the object
with his free hand without having the idea of using the
stick. . . .

[At fourteen months, twenty-five days] I give him back the
stick because of his recent progress. He has learned to put

objects on top of one another, to put them in a cup and turn it upside down, etc.: the relationships that belong to the level of the behavior of the stick. . . . Laurent grasps the stick and immediately strikes the floor with it, then strikes various objects placed on the floor. He displaces them gently, but it does not occur to him to utilize this result systematically. . . . I put various desirable objectives 50 cm or one meter away from Laurent, but he does not realize the virtue of the instrument he holds. . . . If I had repeated such experiments at this period, Laurent, like his sisters, would have discovered the use of the stick through groping and apprenticeship. But I broke off the attempt and only resumed it during the sixth stage.

At sixteen months, five days, Laurent is seated before a table, and I place a bread crust in front of him, well out of reach. Also, to his right I place a stick about 25 cm long. At first Laurent tries to grasp the bread without paying any attention to the instrument, and then he gives up. I then put the stick between him and the bread; it does not touch the bread but nevertheless carries with it an undeniable visual suggestion. Laurent again looks at the bread, without moving, looks very briefly at the stick, then suddenly grasps it and directs it toward the bread. But he grasped it toward the middle, and not at one of its ends, so that it was too short to attain the objective. Laurent then puts it down and resumes stretching out his hand toward the bread. Then, without spending much time on this movement, he takes up the stick again, this time at one of its ends (chance or intention?), and draws the bread to him. He begins by simply touching it, as though contact of the stick with the objective were sufficient to see the latter in motion, but after one or two seconds at most he pushes the crust with real intention. He displaces it gently at first, but then draws it to him without difficulty. Two successive attempts yield the same results. . . . An hour later, I place a toy in front of Laurent (out of his reach) and a new stick next to him. He does not even try to catch the object with his hand; he immediately grasps the stick and draws the toy to him. Thus it may be seen how Laurent has discovered the use of the stick almost without understanding its usefulness. This reaction is therefore distinctively different from that of his sisters. . . .[15]

The reader has undoubtedly noticed that there was in this illustration a gradual development followed by a sudden solution.

But the gradual development is not *of* the solution: Birch's animals did not, during the stick play that followed their initial failure, use the sticks at all to rake objects toward them as required by the problem. What they learned was not a raking response, but a cognitive structure that could be applied to the new situation. The same was true of Laurent.

What happened at the moment of solution was not a cataclysmic change, however. There must have been some sudden change in the brains of Köhler's chimpanzees, and a similar change in Laurent; but Piaget would hold that it was not Köhler's genetically required restructuring of a field, but a new relationship among structures that had been built up previously through countless interactions of the organism with its environment—a "reciprocal assimilation of schemes."

Note that in what Köhler would have called an "insightful solution," the schemes function internally and are relatively independent of sensory input. In the words of Piaget, they do not require "a series of external acts to aliment them continually from without."[16] "The experimentation is interiorized, and coordination takes place before there is external adjustment."[17] (On the other hand, even in the latter half of the Concrete Operations Period the child will be limited in the extent to which he can transcend direct experience, and it is not until the Formal Operations Period that he can deal effectively with "possibilities" as opposed to present realities.)

Object Permanence, Space, and Time

Laurent in Stage 5 had demonstrated object permanence by searching for an object in the place where it had just disappeared. But there the displacements had to be visible. Listen to this episode from Stage 6:

> *Observation 64:*
> [At age nineteen months, twenty days] Jacqueline watches me as I put a coin in my hand, then put my hand under a coverlet. I withdraw my hand closed; Jacqueline opens it, and then finding no coin, she searches under the coverlet till she finds the object.[18]

Piaget then repeats this test by hiding his hand in various other places before dropping the coin, and always with the same result. The child in Stage 5 is unable to follow the displacements of an object unless they are visible. Here, Jacqueline clearly is operating under no such handicap, for she now has "an actual image of the itinerary followed by the object. . . ."[19]

A less formal observation illustrates the same thing:

> *Observation 123:*
> At eighteen months, eight days, Jacqueline throws a ball under a sofa. Instead of bending down at once and searching for it on the floor, she looks at the place, realizes the ball must have crossed under the sofa, and sets out to go behind it. There is a table at her right, and the sofa is backed up against the bed on the left; therefore, she begins by turning her back on the place where the ball disappeared, goes around the table, and finally arrives behind the sofa at the correct place. Thus, she has closed the circle of displacements by an itinerary different from that of the object. . . .[20]

What inferences can you draw from this about the child's conception of space? Perhaps many, but the major change indicated is the increasing importance of internalized symbols in the child's construction of space.

Without going into detail, let me just say that the construction of time has undergone the same transformation as that of space: internal symbols make possible both memory of past events and anticipation of future ones. In Stage 6 the resulting temporal integration encompasses a considerable span.

Causality

Such symbolizing has its effects in every one of the categories explored so far. Causality is no exception.

> *Observation 157:*
> [At eighteen months, eight days] Jacqueline sits on a bed beside her mother. I am at the foot of her bed on the side opposite Jacqueline, and she neither sees me nor knows that I am in the room. I brandish over the bed a cane to which a brush is attached at one end, and I swing the whole thing.

Jacqueline is very much interested: she says "Cane, cane" and examines the swinging most attentively. At a certain moment, she stops looking at the end of the cane and obviously tries to understand. She tries to perceive the other end of the cane, and to do so, leans in front of her mother, and then behind her, until she has seen me. She expresses no surprise, as though she knew I was the cause.[21]

You can see from this illustration that it is now possible for the child to symbolize a *cause* by observing its *effect*. But what about vice versa?

Observation 160:
[At sixteen months, twelve days] Jacqueline has been wrested from a game she wants to continue and placed in her playpen, from which she wants to get out. She calls, but in vain. Then she clearly expresses a certain need, although the events of the last ten minutes prove that she no longer experiences it. No sooner has she left the playpen than she indicates the game she wishes to resume! Thus, we see how Jacqueline, knowing that a certain appeal would not free her from her confinement, has imagined a more efficacious means, foreseeing more or less clearly the sequence of actions that should result from it.[22]

Our subject apparently is capable not only of inferring cause from effect, but also of foreseeing the effect of a cause. Note that both of these are dependent upon the extension of time and space coordinates mentioned earlier; the effect of her action is projected in both. Thus it appears that the extension of time and space that occurs in this stage is accompanied by—and indeed is necessary to—a more sophisticated view of causality.

IMITATION AND PLAY—A SUMMARY

Two categories of activity have so far been deliberately omitted from this analysis of the Sensorimotor Period. They are *imitation* and *play*. The reason for omitting them was not that they are in any way separate from other aspects of development, but rather that it seemed appropriate to close this account of the Sensorimotor Period with a longitudinal summary, and play and imitation lend themselves especially well to that purpose. Together, they can serve as a prototype of all development during this period.

You may recall that Piaget conceives of development as changes in structure through the action of invariant functions. There are just two of those functions,* *assimilation* and *accommodation*, and it happens that *imitation* is nearly pure accommodation and that *play* is almost entirely assimilation.† That is why a longitudinal treatment of these two is particularly instructive and can serve especially well as a review of the period.

STAGE 1 (0–1 MONTH). EXERCISING THE SENSORIMOTOR SCHEMES

Since behavior in this stage is essentially reflexive, there is nothing to say about imitation or play.

STAGE 2 (1–4 MONTHS). PRIMARY CIRCULAR REACTIONS

Imitation

In Stage 2 there are isolated instances of *pseudoimitation*: if someone else does something that the child has just done, the child repeats the pattern. That is not imitation; it is merely assimilation, into an already established scheme, of the other's action as though it were his own.

Nevertheless, Piaget regards pseudoimitation as an intermediate stage in the development of true imitation.

---

*More precisely, he speaks of the invariant functions of *organization* and *adaptation*, with *assimilation* and *accommodation* as subcategories under the latter (see Figure 1.1).

†You may object immediately that much children's play is imitative by its very nature ("playing cowboy," "playing house," etc.). But in those activities the imitative schemes have already been mastered and are currently being assimilated into the play schemes.

Play

Once a primary circular reaction is mastered through combined assimilation and accommodation, it may become "autonomous," so to speak. Piaget cites the example of a Stage 2 child who has learned to throw his head back "to look at familiar things from this new position."[23] Having mastered that pattern, he begins to throw his head back without any apparent attention to what he can see by so doing.

When the accommodation becomes subordinated to the assimilation, and the original "end" of the action drops out, the activity can be classified as play.

STAGE 3 (4–8 MONTHS). SECONDARY CIRCULAR REACTIONS

Imitation

In Stage 3 we find the beginnings of true imitation of sounds and movements that are already in the infant's repertoire. That is, he will often reproduce the actions of another even though he himself has not just previously been engaged in that action.

He reproduces only familiar patterns, however, and his actions still partake as much of assimilation as of accommodation. Moreover, the movements imitated must be visible on his own body.

Play

Although play remains essentially the same as in Stage 2, it is now easier to see the differentiation between play and adaptive assimilation.

An example of the change is the behavior of Lucienne, who discovered early on that she could make the objects hanging from the top of her cot swing. At three and one-half months, she studied this phenomenon seriously, "with an appearance of intense interest." At four months, however, "she never indulged in this activity . . . without a show of great joy and power."[24] The serious work of comprehension, the accommodative aspect of the act, had dropped out entirely; what was left was pure assimilation—i.e., it was play.

STAGE 4 (8–12 MONTHS). COORDINATION OF THE
SECONDARY SCHEMES

Imitation

In Stage 3 the child could imitate only patterns that were already in his own repertoire and those that were visible on his own body. In Stage 4 he is relieved of both those limitations.

Because of the first-named limitation, the Stage 3 child's own actions and those of the model are relatively undifferentiated. Consequently, the imitation is not essentially different from the circular reaction, and the child continues the model's action as though it were his own.

But in Stage 4, as subject and object begin to be differentiated, the child's view of the model's actions is quite different from what it had been previously. "Instead of appearing to be continuations of his own activity, they are now partially independent realities that are analogous to what he himself can do and yet distinct from it."[25] Once that change has occurred, the child develops an interest in novel actions and begins to imitate them.

I cannot help wondering whether the second of the two limitations of Stage 3 would ever be overcome if the child were deprived of the solicitous attention of adults whose imitations of his actions (facial expressions, pointing to various parts of the face, etc.) provide visual feedback correlated with kinesthetic and tactile inputs. I should think that a perpetually present mirror might serve that purpose even better.

Imitation of movements not visible on his own body cannot, like the earlier ones, be interpreted as direct assimilation of the model's behavior pattern into the child's established schema. Rather, it is accomplished by means of transitory "indices," such as a sound associated with a movement of the mouth. The index forms a kind of link—an element common to both patterns— between the visual input from the model and the tacto-kinesthetic input from the child's own movements. When a model says, "Ah," for example, and the child imitates him, the latter gets visual input from the model's open mouth and kinesthetic input from his own. But the child cannot match visual inputs from the two mouths, because he cannot see his own. His open mouth is "linked" to the model's by that which the two agents have in common: the auditory pattern, "Ah."

Play

The distinction between play and adaptive behavior becomes more clear in Stage 4 with the differentiation of means from ends. When the child pursues a means for its own sake he is obviously engaged in play. In the discussion of means-end relations in Stage 4, I referred to the child's attacking a barrier in order to reach a goal object that lay beyond it. When the same child later forgets all about the goal object in his zeal for attacking the barrier, the activity is clearly play.

The pattern called "ritualization" also begins during this stage, but a description of it is deferred until Stage 5.

STAGE 5 (12–18 MONTHS). TERTIARY CIRCULAR REACTIONS

Imitation

The change in Stage 5 is one of degree rather than kind. The child reproduces patterns of the model that are less similar to established schemes, and the reproduction is more precise than it was before.

Play

Stage 5 play is noteworthy for its elaboration of the "ritualization" that first appeared in the previous stage. Whereas Stage 4 rituals were confined to repeating and combining previously established adaptive schemes, in Stage 5 many patterns become games almost immediately, with no intermediate period of adaptive utility.

When Jacqueline's hand slipped from her hair and splashed into the bath water, she repeated the sequence with great glee, varying the heights, as she would if it were a tertiary circular reaction, but always grasping her hair first, which of course had no effect whatever on the ensuing splash.

On another occasion Jacqueline chanced to set an orange peel to rocking on a table immediately after having looked at its convex side, and that became a ritual. She rocked the orange peel at least twenty times, each time looking at its underside before proceeding further.

STAGE 6 (18–24 MONTHS). INVENTION OF NEW MEANS THROUGH MENTAL COMBINATIONS

Imitation

Stage 6 is marked by three advances over the previous one:

1. The child imitates complex new models without extensive trial and error.
2. He imitates nonhuman, even nonliving, objects.
3. He imitates absent objects.

Stage 5 was the era of overt experimentation, and the imitation that occurred there was overtly experimental. But now the experimentation is "interiorized," to use Piaget's term, and the pattern is worked out in his head before he ever does anything that the observer can see.

The imitation of nonhuman objects is important both because it serves the investigator as an indication that representation is going on, and because it can serve the child as the representation itself. When Jacqueline's doll got caught by its feet in the top of her dress, she extricated it, with difficulty; but as soon as she got it out, she tried to put it back again, apparently in an effort to understand what had happened. Failing in this, she crooked her forefinger into the shape of the doll's foot and placed it into the neck of her dress. After pulling briefly with the imprisoned finger, she removed it, apparently satisfied. Piaget interprets this as the construction of "a kind of active representation of the thing that had just happened and that she did not understand."[26]

This mechanism is reminiscent of the "motor meaning" of Stage 3. It is not the same, however, because motor meaning consisted merely of reactivating, in the presence of a particular object, the child's own movements that had previously occurred in the presence of that object, whereas the Stage 6 child reproduces the outline of an action of the *object* (in this example, the doll)—an act that the child herself has never before performed.

The final point about Stage 6 imitation is the main one: the child imitates models that are not physically present at the time of the first reproduction. This so-called *deferred imitation* is consistent with the previously discussed general intellectual characteristics of Stage 6 and is very important in the development of *play*.

Play

The distinctive characteristics of play in Stage 6 can be summed up in a single word: *symbolism*. What had previously been simple motor games are now representations of previous experiences; they are "make-believe."

Lucienne accidentally fell backward while sitting on her cot. Seeing a pillow, she seized it and pressed it against her face as though sleeping on it. Then after a moment she "sat up delightedly." This procedure was repeated many times during the day, even in places other than the cot and with no pillow available. Each time, she would first smile, and then throw herself back and press her hands against her face as though the pillow were there.[27] The symbolic basis of this behavior should be clear to any thoughtful observer.

IMITATION IN THE SERVICE OF PLAY

It is in Stage 6 that play and imitation become fused, with the former dominating the latter. The progress of representational processes in general makes possible the *deferred imitation* that is illustrated by the example cited above and that is an integral part of so much of the play (like the "playing cowboy" and "playing house" mentioned in the footnote on p. 52) that we see in older children. My own term for that relationship is *imitation in the service of play*.

A summary of developments in play and imitation, as well as in all other categories of the analysis, may be found in Table II.

TABLE II. MULTIDIMENSIONAL VIEW OF DEVELOPMENT DURING THE SENSORIMOTOR PERIOD

Stage	Developmental Unit	Intention and Means-end Relations	Meaning	Object Permanence
1	Exercising the Ready-made Sensorimotor Schemes (0–1 mo.)			
2	Primary Circular Reactions (1–4 mo.)		Different responses to different objects	
3	Secondary Circular Reactions (4–8 mo.)	Acts upon objects	"Motor meaning"	Brief single-modality search for absent object
4	Coordination of Secondary Schemes (8–12 mo.)	Attacks barrier to reach goal	Symbolic meaning	Prolonged, multi-modality search
5	Tertiary Circular Reactions (12–18 mo.)	"Experiments in order to see"; discovery of new means through "groping accommodation"	Elaboration through action and feedback	Follows sequential displacements if object in sight
6	Invention of New Means Through Mental Combinations (18–24 mo.)	Invention of new means through reciprocal assimilation of schemes	Further elaboration; symbols increasingly covert	Follows sequential displacement with object hidden; symbolic representation of object, mostly internal

Space	Time	Causality	Imitation	Play
			Pseudo-imitation begins	Apparent functional autonomy of some acts
All modalities focus on single object	Brief search for absent object	Acts; then waits for effect to occur	Pseudo-imitation quicker, more precise. True imitation of acts already in repertoire and visible on own body	More acts done for their own sake
Turns bottle to reach nipple	Prolonged search for absent object	Attacks barrier to reach goal; waits for adults to serve him	True imitation of novel acts not visible on own body	Means often become ends; ritualization begins
Follows sequential displacements if object in sight	Follows sequential displacements if object in sight	Discovers new means; solicits help from adults	True imitation quicker, more precise	Quicker conversion of means to end; elaboration of ritualization
Solves detour problem; symbolic repre-sentation of spatial rela-tionships, mostly internal	Both anticipation and memory	Infers causes from observ-ing effects; predicts effects from observing causes	Imitates (1) complex, (2) non-human, (3) absent models	Treats inade-quate stimuli as if adequate to imitate an enactment —i.e., sym-bolic rituali-zation or "pretending"

NOTES

[1]Jean Piaget, *The Origins of Intelligence in Children*, trans. Margaret Cook (New York: International Universities Press), 1952, pp. 157–159.

[2]*Ibid.*, pp. 186–187.

[3]*Ibid.*, pp. 36ff.

[4]*Ibid.*, pp. 20–21.

[5]*Ibid.*, p. 197.

[6]*Ibid.*, pp. 216–219.

[7]*Ibid.*, p. 249.

[8]Jean Piaget, *The Construction of Reality in the Child*, trans. Margaret Cook (New York: Basic Books, Inc.), 1954, p. 53.

[9]A narrated motion picture taken immediately after the dogs were released can be purchased directly from McGill University, Montreal, Canada. The same events are described in writing by W. R. Thomson and R. Melzack. "Early environment," *Scientific American*, vol. 194, no. 1 (January 1956), pp. 38–42.

[10]Gerald Gratch, Kenneth J. Appel, Wilson F. Evans, Güney K. LeCompte, and Nancy A. Wright, "Piaget's State IV Object Concept Error: Evidence of Forgetting or Object Conception?" *Child Development*, vol. 45, 1974, pp. 71–77.

[11]Piaget, *The Construction of Reality in the Child*, p. 85.

[12]Piaget, *The Origins of Intelligence in Children*, pp. 268–272.

[13]Piaget, *The Construction of Reality in the Child*, p. 67.

[14]Piaget, *The Origins of Intelligence in Children*, pp. 305–306.

[15]*Ibid.*, pp. 33–36.

[16]*Ibid.*, p. 348.

[17]Jean Piaget, *Play, Dreams and Imitation in Childhood*, translated by C. Gattegno and F. M. Hodgson (New York: W. W. Norton & Co., Inc.), 1951.

[18]Piaget, *The Construction of Reality in the Child*, p. 79.

[19]*Ibid.*, p. 82.

[20]*Ibid.*, p. 205.

[21]*Ibid.*, pp. 295–296.

[22]*Ibid.*, p. 297.

[23]Piaget, *Play, Dreams and Imitation in Childhood*, p. 91.

[24]*Ibid.*, p. 92.

[25]*Ibid.*, p. 50.

[26]*Ibid.*, p. 65.

[27]*Ibid.*, pp. 96–97.

Preoperational Period (2-7 years)

Preoperational Period

The essential difference between a child in the Sensorimotor Period and one in the Preoperational Period is that the former is relatively restricted to *direct interactions* with the environment, whereas the latter is capable of manipulating *symbols* that *represent* the environment. As was brought out earlier, however, the foundations of symbolic activity are laid during the Sensorimotor Period.* It was shown that "motor meaning" develops in Stage 3, symbolic meaning in Stage 4, and in Stage 6 even the beginnings of symbol manipulation can be detected.

---

*Piaget is not consistent in his use of the term "symbol." In a single paragraph (*Play, Dreams and Imitation in Childhood*, p. 101) he says of the ritualizations of Stages 4 and 5 that "such actions are certainly not yet properly called symbolic, since the action is only a reproduction of itself and is therefore both signifier and signified," and then refers to those same rituals as "symbols" that serve as a preparation for the "representational symbols" that emerge later on. Perhaps the best recourse here is to place emphasis not on the change toward symbolic representations, but on the increasing differentiations of

ADVANCES

THE SYMBOLIC FUNCTION

The Preoperational child, however, has *signifiers* (words, images, etc.) in his repertoire, and can differentiate them from *significates* (internalized representations of earlier experiences to which the words or images may refer), whereas the Sensorimotor child apparently perceives the sign and its significate as a single unit—e.g., "tinkle-on-bowl-taste-of-soup" or "hat-on-mother-go-away," or even "pillow-thumb-sleep."

During the Sensorimotor Period you will remember that the infant did develop what we called "motor meaning," and that certain events then came to signify other events. The point of making a division here is that the Sensorimotor child can seldom utilize any but concrete signals, whereas the Preoperational child can make an internal response—or a "mediating process," if you prefer—that represents an absent object or event. And he can differentiate the signifier (an internal process that represents tinkle-on-bowl, hat-on-mother, or pillow and thumb-sucking) from the significate (the process that represents taste-of-soup, mother-go-away, or going to sleep).

To summarize, then: entrance into the Preoperational Period is marked by increasing internalization of representational actions and increasing differentiation of signifiers from significates.

ADAPTIVE BEHAVIOR

Intelligence might well be defined as the organization of adaptive behavior, and adaptive behavior is definitely different in the new period.

---

signifiers from significates; though again the issue is clouded, for Piaget sometimes includes the latter in his definition of the former (*Ibid.*, pp 101–102). He also has referred recently to "the period of sensorimotor intelligence" as lasting "until about eighteen months,"[1] possibly in recognition of the appearance of symbolic manipulation in Stage 6.

Action-to-Explanation

The Sensorimotor child is action-oriented; he is limited to the pursuit of concrete goals. The Preoperational child can reflect upon his own behavior—i.e., on the organization of his behavior as it relates to the goal rather than merely on the goal itself (although, as we shall presently see, he does very little reflecting, and he cannot conceive of any other such reflection being different from his own).

Scope

Whereas the Sensorimotor child is limited to linking successive perceptions of concrete objects and events through very *brief* anticipations of the future and memories of the past, the Preoperational child has access to a comprehensive representation of reality that can include past, present, and future and can occur in an exceedingly short period of time. Piaget likens Sensorimotor intelligence to a motion picture both taken and projected very slowly so that "all the pictures are seen in succession, and so without the continuous vision necessary for understanding the whole."[2] The Preoperational child has achieved partial freedom from that limitation (although he is still restricted to representations of states, as distinguished from transformations). (See pp. 74–75.)

Summary

The eventual result of this extension in scope and shift of interest from action to explanation is the development of a system of codified symbols that can be manipulated and communicated to others.

ORIGINS OF THE SYMBOLIC FUNCTION

Accommodation

The symbolic function has a great future; but what about its past? How did it get started? Probably the most important notion here is that of "internalized imitation." Just as absent events were "re-presented" in the Sensorimotor Period by overt imitations triggered by sensory input, so the representation is now accomplished covertly by means of an imitation that has been made in the past and internalized. This, then, is the "signifier": * it signifies the event that was imitated, and it can serve also as a kind of plan for future action.

As an example, do you remember when Jacqueline's doll got caught by its feet on the edge of her blouse? After extricating it, she used her finger to represent the doll's foot as she hooked it into the same place, apparently studying the phenomenon that she had just discovered. She would know what to do, should it happen again. Another example is Lucienne's behavior when confronted with a problem that could be solved by opening a matchbox. The "opening plan" was represented by opening her mouth![3]

Those examples illustrate transitional problem-solving abilities. Later in the Preoperational Period, the motor loops drop out, and the whole process runs itself off without any perceptible movement.

Assimilation

All of what has just been said refers, of course, to accommodation. How does assimilation fit in? Simply by being what it is: the process of signifying *is* essentially an assimilatory process—i.e., it is the process of supplying the significate when the signifier is evoked. Or, to put it another way, the signifier acquires meaning when it is assimilated to the schemes that represent the signified event—i.e., to the corresponding significate.

---

*Two kinds of signifiers differ with respect to their relations to their significates:
  1. "Sign," in which the relation to significate is
     (a) arbitrarily selected and
     (b) socially agreed upon.
  2. "Symbol," in which the significate is
     (a) usually physically similar to signifier and
     (b) private, idiosyncratic.

Coordination of Assimilation and Accommodation

Actually, I have oversimplified this. Piaget classifies functions on the "representative" dimension as follows:

> *Accommodation*
> Effects of the present: simple accommodations.
> Effects of the past: representations and images.
>
> *Assimilation*
> Effects of the present: incorporation of data into adequate schemes.
> Effects of the past: connections established between the present schemes and others whose meanings are merely evoked and not provoked by present perception.[4]

My interpretation of that last effect is that the "others whose meanings are merely evoked" are the "significates" mentioned earlier. (See also pp. 67 and 68.)

The added time dimension is a complication that causes difficulty in the equilibration of assimilation and accommodation, and that, in turn, contributes to the well-known instability of the period, in which the child is continually shifting among play, imitation, and intelligent adaptation.*

But even in deliberately contrived problem-solving situations like the Piagetian "experiments" (e.g., the ones that we shall be examining shortly), the child's adaptation is faulty by adult standards because his cognitive functioning is so unsystematic. There seems to be no metastructure to integrate substructures, so that assimilation of one of the experimenter's displays to one scheme has no necessary implications for any other scheme and hence for the cognition that results from the next display. The outcome in each case is a flagrant logical contradiction—a contradiction that will be corrected when the schemes accommodate to each other as well as to the external environment, thus forming the "metastructure" mentioned above.

---

*One way of conceptualizing at least part of this instability is to think of the child as continually playing games, and that "reality is a game at which he is willing to play with adults and anyone else who believes in it."[5]

SIGNIFIERS, SIGNIFICATES, AND LANGUAGE

Anyone who has ever thought about development has noticed the correlation of verbal ability with the general mental ability of "intelligence." But since correlations are not causes, we are left with the question of what causes what.

Nevertheless, many people have asserted, on the basis of that relation, that "representational thought" results from the learning of words. Piaget does not agree with that view, for he points out that the first signifiers are not linguistic signs, but rather private symbols for which there are no signs.* The shaking of Lucienne's legs represents the bassinet fringe; laying down her head, grasping the blanket, and sucking her thumb represent going to sleep; opening and closing her mouth represent opening and closing a match box; the hooking of Jacqueline's finger around the edge of her blouse represents a doll's foot caught in the same place.

Those are all *imitations*. When the imitations become internalized, Piaget calls them "images," and those images are the first true signifiers. The significates are the complete objects or events being imitated—or rather, their meanings for a particular child.

Identify, if you can, the signifiers and the significates in the following short observation.

> *Observation 77:*
> At twenty-one months Jacqueline saw a shell
> and said "cup." After saying this, she picked it up and
> pretended to drink. (She had often pretended to drink with
> various objects, but in these instances the object was
> assimilated to the drinking schema. Here the identification of
> the shell with the cup preceded the action.) The next day,
> seeing the same shell, she said "glass," then "cup," then
> "hat," and finally "boat in the water." Three days later she
> took an empty box and moved it to and fro saying
> "motycar." . . .[6]

The signifiers are the child's internalized imitations of a shell or a box. The significates are the models of earlier experiences—

---

*See the footnote on page 65 for characteristics of signs and symbols.

the "schemes"—to which the image of the shell or of the box can be assimilated. Another possibility would be for the image of a shell to be assimilated to the concept of a shell—i.e., to a scheme that represents the common features of many "shell experiences" of the past. But in the episode Piaget describes here, the signifier process "shell" is assimilated by the scheme of "cup" in one instance, of "hat" in another, and of "boat" in still another—with some accommodation of each scheme to the image, of course.*

To put it another way, the meanings of the shell consist of the schemes to which it can be assimilated. Words are imitations, too; they serve as signifiers, and their meanings are similarly determined. The words used by Jacqueline in this example refer not to the conventional meaning of "shell," but to the idiosyncratic meanings that reside in this particular subject. Often the referent of a noun is not an object at all, but an action or class of actions. "Mommy" may refer to a large class of helping behaviors, and in certain contexts it means, "Help me!" Or the child may invent words to fit developed concepts. Examples are: "It's raining and winding out." "Let me key the door," or "I can do it 'cause he teached me."

Apparently what the Preoperational child does is to assimilate words into his already established idiosyncratic symbol system.

---

*The signifier process (specific image, internalized imitation) is sometimes called *figurative knowledge;* its transformation into meaning (assimilation to more general structures) is then *operative knowledge.* Used in that way, "operative" is a generic term that refers to the structuring activity of intelligence at any stage of development. The term is not used in this book because it is so susceptible to confusion with our use of the term "operational," which is a subdivision of the "operative" category. (Some writers use the terms interchangeably, apparently assuming that their readers somehow will know when "operational" pertains to "operations" and when it does not. At least one highly respected scholar uses *operational* "in the strict sense" just as we do; but he also uses it "in the wide sense" to include all but sensorimotor actions —which leaves him with the statement that "operational is here taken to include preoperational. . . ."[7])

LIMITATIONS

We have been looking at the Preoperational Period from a perspective gained by first studying the Sensorimotor Period. In short, we have compared this period with the one that preceded it. That is a defensible procedure, of course; but since we are all inclined to take our own intellectual processes for granted, it may be useful to point out ways in which the child's thought is still quite different from that of the adult.

I shall explore those limitations of Preoperational thought under six headings (even though Piaget himself has not done so, and there probably could be many more). The six are:

1) Concreteness
2) Irreversibility
3) Egocentrism
4) Centering
5) States versus transformations
6) Transductive reasoning

Inasmuch as Piaget coined these terms during the course of many years of research and writing, it should not be surprising to find much redundancy in any list of this length. In fact, that is what we do find; in many ways his categories represent different ways of referring to essentially the same thing.

It may be appropriate in the introduction to a section on the inadequacies of preoperational thinking to mention once again that hoary controversy concerning the role of language in thinking. Wordsworth expressed beautifully (as poets are wont to do) one point of view in that regard: "The word," he said, "is not the dress of thought, but its very incarnation."

Not so, says Piaget. Language is the vehicle by which thought is socialized; but it is not the original basis of, nor does it ever become the whole of, human thinking. Our analysis of intellectual development will therefore not be concerned exclusively or even primarily with the development of language. Conversely, the limitations that we shall examine are not primarily linguistic limitations.

CONCRETENESS

You may well be wondering why the Preoperational child is here characterized as "concrete" when the ability to manipulate "symbols" is the main feature that differentiates this period from the one that preceded it. The answer is that compared to the behavior of the Sensorimotor infant, the behavior of the child who has reached the Preoperational Period *is* relatively independent of momentary sensory inputs. But compared to an adolescent or adult, he is still very concrete-minded indeed.

Much of his thinking takes the form of what Piaget calls *mental experiment*. Instead of the adult pattern of analyzing and synthesizing, the Preoperational child simply runs through the symbols for events as though he were actually participating in the events themselves. That has implications for the next category in the list, the very important characteristic that Piaget calls "irreversibility."

IRREVERSIBILITY

"Reversible" means "capable of being returned to its point of origin"; every mathematical or logical operation is reversible. For example:

$$3 + 5 = 8, \text{and}$$
$$8 - 5 = 3.$$

Or

all men and all women = all adults, and
all adults except women = all men.

You can

add something to the "3" and then
take it away.

You can

increase the size of the group, and then
decrease it again.

In each case, you have

thought your way from one condition to another, and then
returned to the starting point.

That is the defining characteristic of reversible thought. It is *not* a characteristic of the thought of a Preoperational child.

Note also that each of these changes is a part of a closed system in which any change in one part of the system requires a compensating change in some other part. For example:

> if 3 + 5 = 8 and
> I increase the "3" by one,
> I must also decrease the "5" by the same amount if I am
> to stay within the system—i.e., the system of two numbers
> whose sum is "8."

It is of course not surprising that the Preoperational child cannot accomplish this reversal; after all, he hasn't been yet taught arithmetic. But here is a problem that does not demand such special skill:

Two plasticene balls of equal size are shown to a child. He is asked,

> "Are they the same size, or
> does one have more plasticene in it than the other?"

He says they are the same. Then—right before his very eyes—one of the balls is rolled into a sausage shape and he is asked the same question as before. This time he says that one has more plasticene than the other! Usually he says the sausage is the

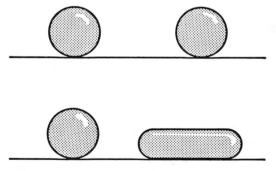

Figure 3.1

larger, but sometimes it is the ball. In Piaget's terms, he fails to *conserve* "substance"*—i.e., he fails to continue to think of the amount of clay as the same while its length and width are changing.

Why should a transformation performed entirely within his visual field and with his full attention produce such a result? One reason is that the child's thinking cannot reverse itself back to the point of origin. He can "see" neither (1) that since nothing has been either added or removed, the sausage could be made back into the original ball, nor (2) that every change in height is compensated by a change in breadth, leaving the total quantity what it was in the beginning. Those failures constitute two kinds of irreversibility.

Another example very similar to the plasticene-ball problem consists of comparing two equal amounts of liquid or two equal numbers of wooden beads in containers of different shape. Let us assume that beads are used.†

The child is given a pile of beads; he is then asked to pick up one in each hand,

> to put the one in the left hand into Container *A*,
> to put the one in the right hand into Container *B*, and
> to continue until there are no more pairs to pick up.

But Containers *A* and *B* are differently shaped, as shown in Figure 3.2. And when the subject is asked, "Which has the larger number of beads,

> Container *A* or
> Container *B*; or
> do they both contain the same amount?"

his answer is, "There's more in this one," and he points sometimes to *A*, but usually to *B*. (Just which one it is depends upon

---

*"Substance" is sometimes called "mass," sometimes "matter," sometimes simply "quantity."

†This makes it a test of conservation of discontinous rather than of continous quantity. I shall nevertheless refer henceforth to both of these problems (beads and liquid) together as "the water-level problem."[8]

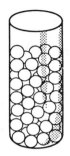

CONTAINER *A*   CONTAINER *B*

Figure 3.2

"centering,"[9] which will soon be discussed. Occasionally a subject will make his judgment on the basis not of one or the other dimension of the material itself but of the sizes of the containers: "This one has more because the jar is bigger." It is as though the child's internal representations of quantities of materials are assimilated into his representation of the containers that hold them. (See the discussion of "transductive reasoning" on pages 75–78.)

The young child makes what to us are startling errors in thinking even about simple transpositions that occur within his field of vision. He does so mainly because his thinking is *not reversible*.

EGOCENTRISM

Just as the early Sensorimotor child was "egocentric" in his overt actions ("the world is my actions upon it"), so the Preoperational child is egocentric in his representations ("the world is as it looks to me").

The term "egocentric" is used not in a pejorative sense, but descriptively, to refer to his inability to take another person's point of view. He will speak to you using words that have idiosyncratic referents and using associations unrelated to any discernible logical structure; and then he'll be very much surprised when he fails to communicate. He is surprised because he cannot understand how you can see it any way but his way.

The ability to take the view of the other (without losing his own) and the corresponding social norm of logical consistency will be acquired partly as by-products of the child's construction of a well-articulated model of the physical world *via* myriad interactions with that world—a model characterized by stable *relationships* among objects. But it will be dependent also upon repeated social interactions in which the child is compelled again and again to take account of the viewpoints of others. This social feedback is extremely important in developing the capacity to think objectively about his own thinking, without which logic is impossible.

CENTERING

Related to all the preceding characteristics is the one called "centering," or "centration."[10] It refers to the child's tendency to center his attention on one detail of an event and hence his inability to process information from other aspects of the situation. That inability is characteristic of the Preoperational child, and it has a disturbing effect on his thinking, as you may well imagine.

In the water-level problem, for example, he will center on either the height of the container (and say that the tall one is larger) or the width (and say that the wide one is larger). If it were possible for him to decenter in this problem, he could take into account both the height and the width, and that would allow him to relate the changes in one of those dimensions to compensatory changes in the other.

But the Preoperational child cannot decenter, and—at least partly for that reason—cannot solve the problem.

STATES VERSUS TRANSFORMATIONS

Also related to deployment of attention is the Preoperational child's tendency to focus on the successive *states* of a display rather than on the *transformations* by which one state is changed into another. Looking at the water-level problem with this tendency in mind, it is easy to see how it might hinder the child's thinking. The transformation by itself would give an adult a feeling of certainty that the water poured from one beaker to another is the same water. But it doesn't do that for the child. It is as though he were viewing a series of still pictures instead of the movie that the adult sees.

A dramatic illustration of this comes from an experiment in which the subject's task was "to depict (by actual drawings or by multiple-choice selection of drawings) the successive movements of a bar that falls from a vertical, upright position to a horizontal one."[11] A correct sequence would look something like that shown in Figure 3.3. That sequence is of course obvious

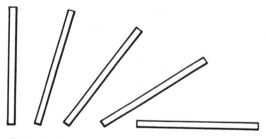

Figure 3.3

to an adult, but the young child commonly fails to draw the intermediate positions of the stick—or sometimes even to recognize them when they are shown to him.

Preoperational children have much difficulty with this simple —and, to an adult, obvious—action sequence. They are unable to integrate a series of states or conditions into a coherent whole —namely, a *transformation*.

TRANSDUCTIVE REASONING

During the Sensorimotor Period we noted the gradual development of a conception of causality. Transitional between that and the reasoning of the adult is what Piaget calls "preconceptual" or "transductive" reasoning. Since Piaget is a logician as well as a psychologist, I prefer not to argue with him when he calls it "reasoning," but it certainly doesn't follow the familiar rules we know as reason. Instead of proceeding from the particular to the general (induction), or from the general to the particular (deduction), the Preoperational child proceeds from particular to particular (transductive reasoning).

The result is sometimes a correct conclusion, as it was when Jacqueline, at thirty months, twenty-seven days said:

"Daddy's getting hot water, so he's going to shave."[12] But sometimes it is rather strange:

> *Observation 111:*
> At two years, fourteen days, Jacqueline wanted a doll-dress that was upstairs: she said *"Dress,"* and when her mother refused to get it, "Daddy get dress." As I also refused, she wanted to go herself "To mommy's room." After several repetitions of this she was told that it was too cold there. There was a long silence, and then: "Not too cold." [I asked] "Where?" "In the room." "Why isn't it too cold?" "Get dress."[13]

The reader may object that this is merely common childish insistence on getting what he wants. That may be true, but it is just that common childish behavior that Piaget is trying to explain—or at least to classify. The fact is that childish insistence is qualitatively different from adult insistence. Piaget characterizes the child's thinking in this example as "a continuation, in a slightly more complicated form, of the practical coordinations of the baby of twelve to sixteen months—e.g., rolling a watch chain into a ball to make it go into a box, etc. . . ."[14] The baby used a sensorimotor coordination as a means to an end; the young child uses mental coordinations. It is important to note here that I said "mental," not "verbal" coordinations. Jacqueline is not manipulating her speech in order to manipulate her parents. She actually *believes* what she says; the thoughts themselves have been recruited to the service of a goal.

In one of the above examples, the child's so-called "reasoning" led to a correct conclusion; in the other, it did not. But in either case, the same plan was followed, namely:

> A causes B is not different from
> B causes A.
> "Daddy's shave requires hot water" is not different from
> "Hot water requires Daddy's shave."
> "A warm room makes possible the fetching of a dress" is not different from
> "The fetching of the dress makes the room warm."

Another, somewhat different, pattern that is also called "transductive reasoning" concerns the child's lack of a hierarchy of categories. Adults can comprehend, for example, a hierarchy like the one depicted in Figure 3.4.*

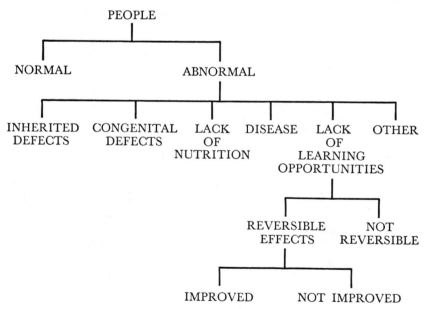

Figure 3.4

---

*Some Formal Operations adults fumble this one badly—e.g., when they categorize as genetically inferior a minority group whose members have lacked

But here is Jacqueline, dealing with a similar hierarchy:

Observation 112:
At twenty-five months, thirteen days, Jacqueline wanted to see a little hunchbacked neighbor whom she used to meet on her walks. A few days earlier she had asked why he had a hump, and after I had explained she said: "Poor boy, he's ill, he has a hump." The day before, Jacqueline had also wanted to go and see him, but he had influenza, which Jacqueline called being "ill in bed." We started out for our walk and on the way Jacqueline said: "Is he still ill in bed?" "No. I saw him this morning, he isn't in bed now." "He hasn't a big hump now!"[15]

Figure 3.5 shows the hierarchical pattern that must be built up in a person's mind before he can deal effectively with this type of problem. Jacqueline blithely transfers "recovery" in *A* to recovery in *B*, because her thinking lacks that hierarchical structure.

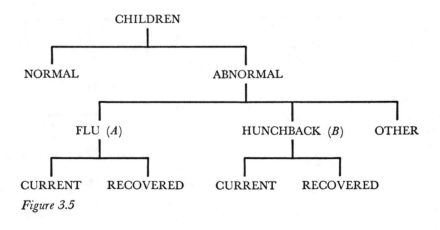

Figure 3.5

learning opportunities. But Formal Operations adults are intellectually capable of doing better than that.

The reasoning is by simile:

> A is like B in some way; therefore
> A is like B in every way.*

Or to put it another way (and this is roughly the way Piaget puts it)[16]; A is *assimilated* into B. The child is *centering* on B, and until he can decenter, his thinking will be characterized by a notable coarseness and rigidity—a lack of refinement and mobility—as compared to the operational thinking of the Concrete Operations Period.

SUMMARY

The infant's world consists entirely of his own actions; objects exist only as aliments to his motor schemes. The Preoperational child lives in a more stable world, in that it is populated by the permanent objects that he constructed during his Sensorimotor Period, and he can deal mentally with both past and future events as well as present ones.

But the *relations* that he establishes among those objects and events are *not* so stable. They form only the beginnings of an equilibrated system for processing information about concrete reality. That system is brought to near perfection during the next period of development: the one called "Concrete Operations."

---

*Again, this a fairly accurate picture of the rigidity that can be found in the thinking of many adults in certain situations (e.g., A and B both have dark skins; B is shiftless and irresponsible; therefore, so is A). Piaget has not dealt extensively with the question of why adult structures are not always used.

NOTES

[1]Jean Piaget, *The Child and Reality: Problems of Genetic Psychology* (New York: Viking Press, 1973), p. 12.

[2]The official translation likens Sensorimotor intelligence to "a slow-motion film," but in a context that I believe clearly justifies my version. Jean Piaget, *The Psychology of Intelligence*, trans. M. Piercy and D. E. Berlyne (London: Routledge and Kegan Paul Ltd., 1950), p. 121. [Original French edition, 1947.]

[3]Jean Piaget, *Play, Dreams and Imitation in Childhood*, trans. C. Gattegno and F. M. Hodgson (New York: W. W. Norton & Co., Inc.), 1951, p. 65.

[4]*Ibid.*, p. 241.

[5]*Ibid.*, p. 93.

[6]*Ibid.*, p. 124.

[7]Hans G. Furth, *Piaget and Knowledge* (Englewood Cliffs, New Jersey: Prentice-Hall), 1969, p. 263.

[8]Jean Piaget and Alina Szeminska, *The Child's Conception of Number*, trans. C. Gattegno and F. M. Hodgson (New York: Humanities Press, Inc.), 1952, p. 25ff.

[9]Bärbel Inhelder, "Criteria of Stages of Mental Development," *in* Tanner and Inhelder (eds.), *Discussions on Child Development* (New York: International Universities Press), 1960, pp. 75–85.

[10]*Ibid.*

[11]Reported by Piaget in *Bull. Psychol.*, Paris, 1959, and cited by Flavell in his *The Developmental Psychology of Jean Piaget* (Princeton: D. Van Nostrand Co., Inc.), 1963, p. 158. The words are Flavell's.

[12]*Play, Dreams and Imitation in Childhood*, 1951. pp. 230–231.

[13]*Ibid.*

[14]*Ibid.*, p. 233.

[15]*Ibid.*, p. 231.

[16]*Ibid.*, p. 235.

Concrete Operations Period (7-11 years)

4

Concrete Operations
Period

In at least one place, Piaget has defined an "operation" as "an action that can return to its starting point, and that can be integrated with other actions also possessing this feature of reversibility."[1] But an additional restriction should be included in the definition: the action is internalized. Flavell says that "any *representational* act that is an integral part of an organized network of related acts is an operation."[2] And finally, the resulting structures "give rise to a feeling of intrinsic necessity."[3] The reason for calling this new period "*concrete* operations" will become clear presently.

In discussing the Preoperational Period, I compared the cognitive processes of that period with those of the periods that precede and follow it. I shall be using a similar approach in this chapter to compare Preoperational functioning with Concrete

Operational functioning in each of several different kinds of problems.

> Classification
> Conservation of quantity: substance, weight, and volume
> Conservation of number
> Numbering
> Egocentrism in the representation of objects
> Egocentrism in social relations
> Egocentrism in reasoning
> Estimating water lines
> Distance, time, movement, and velocity

Actually, more time will be given, in the section on "problems," to Preoperational functioning than to Concrete Operational functioning, for there is no better way to develop an understanding and appreciation of the latter than to contrast it with the former. The various qualities of thought that have been discussed, and some that have not, will manifest themselves in the solutions to those problems.

Before proceeding with the problems, however, it might be useful to provide an additional framework for discussion by pointing out that with the Concrete Operations Period, Piaget's emphasis shifts to examining the relations between thinking and symbolic logic, and by sketching briefly the properties of the "groupings" of "concrete operations" that characterize this period of development. The rules of mathematics and logic are widely used by psychologists to govern their own behavior as scientists, but Piaget uses them as models of the mental functioning of children. He is convinced that the rules of logic have developed, both philogenetically and ontogenetically, as a result of the exigencies of living in a lawful universe. The actions that were first overt, and then internalized, now begin to form tightly organized *systems* of actions. Any internal act that forms an integral part of one of those systems Piaget calls an "operation." "Preoperational," "concrete operational," and "formal operational" describe different levels of systematic mental activity.

The actions implied by the mathematical symbols listed below are all examples of operations.[4]

+ combining
− separating
× repeating
÷ dividing
> placing in order
= possible substitution

These have their counterparts in logic: e.g., "and" represents the action of *combining*; "except" represents the action of *separating*. Thus the structures of logic may be used to represent the structures of thought; the one serves as a model for the other.

That does not mean that people always think that way, but Piaget believes that any subject who ever thinks that way has a cognitive structure that can be represented in logical terms. Any other kind of thinking is regarded as a failure either to use a developed structure or to develop the structure in the first place.

PROPERTIES OF GROUPS AND GROUPINGS

In the Concrete Operations Period, structures often take the form that Piaget calls "groupings." A grouping is a system of operations that combines attributes of both the *group* and the *lattice*.[5]

THE GROUP

A group is a system that consists of a set of elements and an operation on those elements such that the following principles apply:

Composition (sometimes called *closure* or *combinativity*): The result of every operation (remember that an operation is an action

that is part of a system of actions) is itself a part of the system.*
For example, if

$$A \circ B = C,$$

C is a part of the system as well as A and B.

Associativity: When the operation is performed within the system,

$A \circ (B \circ C)$ is the same as
$(A \circ B) \circ C$;

combining A with the result of combining B and C is the same as combining C with the result of combining A and B.

Identity: In every system there is one and only one element that, when combined with other elements in the system, leaves the result unchanged. It is called the *identity element*.

$A \circ I = A$, and
$I \circ A = A$,

where I is the identity element.

For example,

if the operation were multiplication, I would be 1;
if it were addition, I would be 0.

Reversibility: For every element there is another that negates it. The negating element, called an *inverse*, is the only one that, when combined with the first element, yields the identity element.

$$A \circ A' = I,$$

where A' is the inverse of A.

If the operation were addition, the inverse would be $(-A)$;
if it were multiplication, the inverse would be $(1/A)$.

---

*The symbol ∘ here represents the operation. Addition and multiplication of integers are examples.

Here is a set of elements:

1   2   3   4   5   6   7   8   9

Let us say that the operation is addition. Is this set a group? The way to find out is to check it against the four properties described above, namely:

> *Composition:* The product (sum) of 8 and 9, for example, is 17, which is not within the system.
>
> *Associativity:* $(2 + 4) + (6 + 8) = 2 + (4 + 6) + 8 = 2 + 4 + (6 + 8)$, or any other example you may choose.
>
> *Identity:* There is no identity element in the set.
>
> *Reversibility:* There is no inverse.

The set meets only one of the criteria; it is not a group unless it meets all four.* What if the set were changed to include all positive and negative integers plus zero?

> *Composition:* The sum of any two or more integers yields an integer. $3 + 5 + 9 = 17$.
>
> *Associativity:* It matters not whether the sum of 3 and 5 is added to 9 or 3 is added to the sum of 5 and 9.
>
> *Identity:* Adding zero doesn't change anything.
>
> *Reversibility:* For each positive integer there is a negative that cancels it. $3 + (-3) = 0$.

This one does have all the properties of a group.†

It should perhaps be mentioned that even sensorimotor equilibrium can involve group structure. If each of the corners of the triangular block in Figure 4.1 were perceptually distinctive, a two-year-old child would be able to keep track of his own displacements of the object, including rotary ones. Those displacements would form a sensorimotor (sometimes called "practical") group; when a subject can predict the positions that will

---

*It is a lattice, however. See pages 88–90.

†It also has all properties of a lattice.

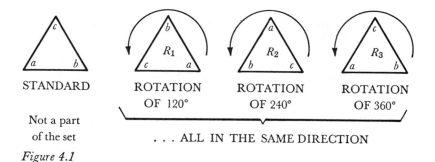

STANDARD ROTATION OF 120° ROTATION OF 240° ROTATION OF 360°

Not a part of the set

. . . ALL IN THE SAME DIRECTION

Figure 4.1

result from various relations, his cognition is said to be *operational*. If a Concrete Operational subject is predicting the positions of the block in Figure 4.1, his thinking will exhibit the following qualities:

Composition: The product of any two or more of the possible rotations is also one of them.

$$R_1 \circ R_1 = R_2,$$
$$R_1 \circ R_2 = R_3,$$
$$R_1 \circ R_3 = R_1.$$

Associativity: Given a specific set of rotations, it does not matter in what combination the operations are performed.

$$(R_2 \circ R_2) \circ R_1 = R_1 \circ R_1 = R_2,$$
$$R_2 \circ (R_2 \circ R_1) = R_2 \circ R_3 = R_2.$$

Identity: Because R_3 returns to its point of origin, it is the identity element in the set.

Reversibility: R_1 is the inverse of R_2 and vice versa, because their resultant is R_3, the identity element.

The Sensorimotor group is a model of the structure of *overt actions*; the Formal Operations group is concerned with propositions, as described in Chapter 5 (though the mathematical modeling of formal thought is too intricate to be treated adequately in a text of this kind, and no attempt will be made to do so); the Concrete Operational group combines with the lattice to model the qualities of thinking that are of primary concern in this chapter.

THE LATTICE

A lattice is a structure consisting of a set of elements and a relation that can encompass two or more of those elements. Specifically, that relation must be such that any two elements have one *least upper bound* (l.u.b.) and one *greatest lower bound* (g.l.b.). The least upper bound of two elements is the smallest element that includes them both. If element B includes element A, then the l.u.b. of A and B is B. In a hierarchy of classes, for example, if Class B includes A as a subclass, the l.u.b. of A and B is B (see Fig. 4.2). Similarly, the greatest lower bound is the largest

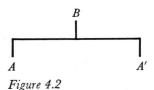

Figure 4.2

element that is included in both. Since A is included both in itself and in B, but B is included in itself only, the g.l.b. of A and B is A.

Here is a set of elements:

  1 2 3 4 5 6 7 8 9

Again, the operation is addition. Is the set a lattice? Take 5 and 8, for example:

> 8 is the smallest element that includes both (l.u.b.), and
> 5 is the largest element that is included in both (g.l.b.).

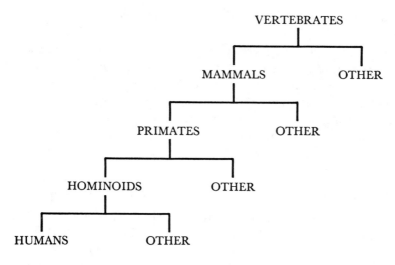

Figure 4.3

Figure 4.3 shows another set of elements, this one arranged in a class hierarchy. Can you find an l.u.b. and a g.l.b. for any pair of these elements?

Take the pair "vertebrate-mammal," for example:

> *Vertebrate* is the smallest class that includes both classes, and *mammal* is the largest class that is included in both.

Other possible two-element relations are: mammal-primate, primate-hominoid, and hominoid-human. Since in any one of those it is possible to find both an l.u.b. and a g.l.b., this hierarchy is therefore a lattice. As a matter of fact, the lattice seems to be a particularly useful device for representing logical classes and relations in hierarchical form,* though it also is used to model

---

*Piaget himself uses a hierarchy of classes to illustrate the properties of a lattice. It might better be called a "semilattice," however; because although all the vertical relations in the diagrams (*A*, *B*, and *C*, etc.) meet the requirements of a lattice, the horizontal ones (*A* and *A'*, *B* and *B'*, *C* and *C'*, etc.) do not. The members of a horizontal pair are exclusive classes by definition.

the so-called combinatorial analysis of formal thought, in which the outcomes are propositions or statements of possibilities rather than the tangible realities that concern the Concrete Operational child. It should be noted in this regard that to qualify as models of concrete operations, the contents processed by each structure must be just that—concrete. Later on, the adolescent will be able to formulate an abstract definition of, say, a "mammal" or a "primate"; but at this stage he works with concrete exemplars of each class.

THE GROUPING

We have now had a brief look at the properties of *groups* and of *lattices*. *Groupings* include aspects of them both. Nine distinct groupings make their appearance during the Concrete Operations Period. Describing them all would be beyond the scope of this book, but fortunately the first one ("Grouping I") illustrates the basic characteristics of all of them. Grouping I (see Fig. 4.4),

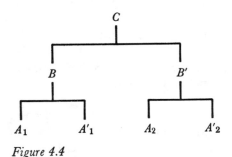

Figure 4.4

Primary Addition of Classes, is concerned with class hierarchies of the form $A + A' = B$, $B + B' = C$, etc., where A is an independently defined category and A' comprises "all the B that is not A." For example, if A were "human" and B were "humanoids," A' would be "chimpanzee, gibbon, gorilla, and orangutan." *Posing* ("setting up" or "thinking of") a class is logical *addition; unposing* ("excluding" or "omitting") is *subtraction*. The nature of the hierarchy becomes apparent when we add two subordinate classes:

Posing both A and A' is the equivalent of posing B.
Posing B and B' together is the same as posing C.

Conversely,

$B - A = A'$, and $B - A - A' = 0$.

Using the notation just presented, turn back to Figure 4.3 and note that if the class "humans" were designated as A, then "hominoids" would be B, "primates" C, "mammals" D,. and "vertebrates" E.

Now try translating the equations given on pages 90 and 91 into the more concrete terms of the zoological classification:

$A + A' = B$, for example, becomes humans + anthropoid apes = all hominoids;
$B + B' = C$ is now hominoids + monkeys, lemurs, etc. = all primates;
$B - A = A'$ becomes hominoids − humans = anthropoid apes;
$B - A - A' = 0$ is now hominoids − humans − anthropoid apes = an empty or null class.

The grouping has, by virtue of its kinship with the group, a *general identity element*, which, as you will recall, "when combined with other elements in the system, leaves the result unchanged." But in addition to general identity the grouping has, by virtue of its kinship to the lattice, a *special identity element*—or rather, "elements," for there is a pair of them:

1) *Tautology* $A + A = A$. (The class "humans" when combined with the class "humans" yields the class "humans.")
2) *Resorption:* $A + B = B$; $A + C = C$; etc. (Humans combined with hominoids yields hominoids; humans combined with primates yields primates; etc.)

The special identity element in each of these is A—in this example, the class "humans."

These are but a few of the many examples that could be given; many more could be generated by the single hierarchy depicted in Figure 4.3. They would all have characteristics of both group and lattice,* but Piaget believed that, for the most part, children's behavior is consonant with neither the group nor the lattice as such; so he formulated a hybrid, the grouping, as a more adequate model of their thinking.

At this point I am constrained to make a comment that may either anger or relieve the reader, depending on how meticulously he has worked to master the material so far presented. My comment is this: It is not the details of the system presented here that are important; what is important is *the idea of system itself*. Piaget does not conceive of responses being connected to stimuli as the child develops, but rather of actions being related to other actions within a *system* of actions. In the Concrete Operations Period, any change in one part of that system has implications for other parts.

SOME REPRESENTATIVE PROBLEMS

With the properties of groupings in mind, let us proceed to analyze as best we can the behavior of children who are faced with the various kinds of problems that were mentioned in the introduction to this chapter.

CLASSIFICATION[6]

When the child achieves true classification, he is able to differentiate and to coordinate two crucial properties of a "class": *intention* and *extension*.

---

*But they would not have all those characteristics. When this class hierarchy was presented as a lattice (p. 89), I pointed out that it did not have all the properties thereof. The same must be said of it as a group, for $B - A - A'$ lacks associativity; $(B - A) - A' = 0$, but does $B - (A - A')$? Actually, A' cannot be subtracted from A at all, because the two are exclusive categories.

"Intention" is the criterion—the quality that defines the class. "Extension" is the sum of all the objects that meet that criterion. The intention of the class "square cards" in Figure 4.5 would be "squareness," and its extension would be "four." Other possible classes from the display in Figure 4.5 are:

> intention "roundness," extension "five";
> intention "black," extension "seven"; and
> intention "white," extension "two."

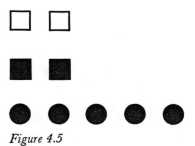

Figure 4.5

In any fully equilibrated classification system, intention and extension must be completely coordinated. The intention of a class determines what objects may be included within it, and the objects that *are* in any collection impose severe limits on the attributes that *might* be used as criteria for classification.

Preoperational

The early Preoperational child is not yet capable of such coordination. He has had much experience with objects of many different kinds, and he has become aware of many attributes of those objects; but he is easily distracted by the *configuration* of an array, and even while he is actually working from a "similarities" base, he often includes objects that do not meet the class criterion, and he frequently changes the criterion.

When he is presented with a display like the one in Figure 4.6 and is asked to "put together those that are alike," the child

Figure 4.6

may begin by placing objects together that are alike in one way, then continue doing the same thing, but using a different attribute. He might begin sorting by shape and suddenly switch to color. Then, when he is halfway through, he may notice that his arrangement looks like a tree. After that, he will add objects in such a manner as to make it look more like a tree, completely ignoring both shape and color. Or he may group the objects on what appears to be a completely random basis (possibly because the child's criteria change so rapidly that no sorting at all is discernable to the adult observer). And finally, he may simply *omit* some objects from *all* of his collections.

Sometimes he *seems* to be using a classification strategy even when his mental functioning actually falls far short of that achievement. Wouldn't you be tempted to interpret the arrangement in Figure 4.7 in that way if your subject had constructed it by himself? That is, wouldn't you call it a product of "classification?" You would until you heard him say, "Choo choo." [!]

Figure 4.7

In that instance, his vocalizing gave him away, but even a child this young often will speak as though he comprehends important extensional concepts like "some" and "all." He may use the words with no hesitation; but, as will be shown, careful testing reveals that he lacks the clearly defined ideas to which they refer when an adult uses them.

For the early Preoperational child, a given intention does not determine any specific *extension*. He may begin putting *black* cards together but leave out some blacks and finally throw in some *non*blacks; or he may appear to move the cards completely at random.

Later in the Preoperational Period he does much better. He siezes upon a single attribute and sticks to it, and he applies it to *all* objects in the array. He may even set up what appears to be a *hierarchy* of categories of the type $A + A' = B$.

In Figure 4.6, A might be "white squares," and A' "black squares"; then B would be "squares," and B' would be "circles." Or A could be "circular blacks," and A' "square blacks"; then B would be "blacks," and B' would be "whites."

The child's arrangement might look just like Figure 4.5. Why, then, is Piaget reluctant to credit this child with true classification? The reason is that the subject's thinking still lacks the *inclusion relation*. Given the array of cards depicted in Figure 4.5, here is a simple test[7] that will prove it:

> E: "I'll take away the two white square cards and put them over here. (E removes two cards from the display depicted in Figure 4.5.) Now, if I were to take away all the *round* ones, would there be any cards left?"
> S: "Yes, the squares."
> E: "If I should take away all the *black* ones, would there be any cards left?"
> S: "No."
> E: Which would make the bigger pile of cards, the round ones or the black ones?"
> S: "The round ones." [!]

That surely is a surprising response, from an adult point of view. It is surprising because adult thinking depends upon structures that the Preoperational child does not have. In this example, an adequate structure might be something like that depicted in Figure 4.8.

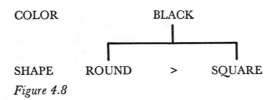

Figure 4.8

According to the principle of composition, the class of black cards is part of the system that includes the round ones and the square ones, but for the Preoperational child that is not so. His approach to the problem is characterized by *centering* (on the shape dimension), *irreversibility* (from the parts back to the whole whence they came), and *transductive reasoning* (a part-to-part relation that excludes the part-to-whole relation). In those circumstances, it is impossible for him truly to comprehend the concepts "some" and "all."

Concrete Operations

According to Piaget, the faultless performances of the late Preoperational child in his other interactions with this array are indicative not of a *classificatory operation*, but merely of a "momentary differentiation of the collection of B into subcollections A and A'."[8]

An "operation" is by definition *reversible*, and it is not until somewhat later that the child is capable

> not only of the *union*, $A + A' = B$,
> but also of its *inverse*, $A = B - A'$,
> or to put it another way, $B - A' = A$, which is where he started.

A Preoperational "collection" (B) ceases to exist when its sub-classes are separated—either in space or only in thought, as they are when their extensions are compared. The Concrete Operations "class" (also B in the equation) is stable and permanent; it will not disintegrate under any conditions.

CONSERVATION OF QUANTITY: SUBSTANCE, WEIGHT, AND VOLUME

Other problems are used to assess conservation of substance, weight, and volume. The term *conservation* refers to the subject's realization that certain properties (in this section, quantity of material) of a system remain the same in spite of transformations (of length and width) performed within the system. The meaning of the term "quantity" in common speech is clear only in con-text; the same is true here. In this section, when the term "quantity of substance" (or simply "substance") is used, it refers to the amount of space occupied by the object, as judged by the child while he is looking at the object and only at the object; later, that same occupied space will be inferred from the amount of water displaced by the object and will be called "volume." "Weight" is what might be expected—namely, the effect that the object has on the movement of a balance. The plasticene-balls problem, cited earlier (p. 71), can be used as an example of conservation of quantity; let us first review the reaction of the Preoperational child to that problem and then compare it with that of the child in the Concrete Operations Period.

Preoperational

One very important characteristic of the conservational structure is *reversibility* (see page 70). Notice in Figure 4.9 that the third-order classification (width) is not a mere duplicate of the first and second (quantity and length); its freedom is restricted. If the quantity is the same (the special condition of conservation) and the length is smaller, the width cannot be "smaller," "same," or "larger"; it can only be larger. Similarly, if the length is

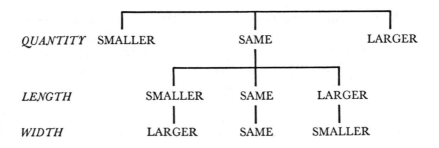

Figure 4.9

larger, the width can only be smaller. The usual term for this special feature of conservation is *reciprocity*. It is one of two kinds of reversibility; the other is *inversion* (sometimes called negation), or thinking one's way back to the original state of the display—in this example, to two balls of equal size.

The Preoperational child cannot conserve at all. If the experimenter rolls the ball into a sausage right before the subject's eyes, the child will say that it becomes larger (or sometimes smaller) than the comparison ball. Refer to the list of limitations on page 69 for the reasons. Again, *centering, states vs. transformation, irreversibility,* and *transductive reasoning* seem especially appropriate. And all of those limitations may be conceived as a lack of mobility within a classes-and-relations structure.

The "sausage" can be classified as smaller than, the same as, or greater than the ball. But that classification can be done on at least three bases: quantity, length, and width. (Depth, an obvious fourth one, will be omitted for the sake of simplicity.)

Figure 4.9 shows those relations. Remember that it represents a structure that the Preoperational child has not yet developed. He cannot move easily from one to another part of the figure in accordance with the rules implicit in it (always follow the lines). Instead, he centers on one dimension (length or width) and on the end-state rather than the transformation—an end-state that he blithely transfers from one dimension to another. Furthermore, he is committed to that end-state; he cannot mentally reverse the transformation and arrive back at "same quantity," either by using the gain in width to compensate for the loss in height (reciprocity) or by mentally undoing both (inversion). Surely reversibility must make an important contribution to the autonomy of central processes that was discussed in Chapter 1. Without such autonomy, children are dominated by their perceptions.

Perceptual domination can be demonstrated even in adults, under special conditions. Such conditions do, in fact, obtain in Figure 4.10. The best way of demonstrating that is to administer to yourself the following brief psychomotor test:

> Place the butt end of a pencil or a pen within the alley at the very top of Figure 4.10. Your object is to reach the center of the spiral as quickly as possible without leaving that alley. Now look at your watch, note carefully what the time will be at the next even minute, and then, at exactly the time you have noted, begin.

Figure 4.10

How long did it take? Did you finish? If not, then you are now in a position to *think* of this figure as a series of concentric circles instead of a spiral. Having taken the prescribed "test," your thinking is no longer dominated by your perception; but you still can *perceive* it in only one way.

The Preoperational child is as unable to process information from the molded plasticene as "same quantity" as you were initially unable to process information from Figure 4.10 as "concentric circles." In both child and adult, *perception* is the dominant mental acitivity. The difference between them is that when you discovered that the path did not lead to the center, you *could* conceptualize the figure in those terms; that is, your mental processes exhibited mobility within a conceptual structure. The Preoperational child cannot; his thinking lacks that mobility, because it lacks that structure.

Concrete Operations

When he *can* think in ways that contradict his immediate impression, he has moved into the Concrete Operations Period. At about the age of seven, he conserves substance but denies that the *weight* remains the same when a plasticene ball is molded into a sausage. Later (at around nine years of age), he conserves *weight* but not *volume*.* Each acquisition represents for its own attribute—whether that is substance, weight, volume, or some other—an *invariance* similar to the one that the child achieved in his Sensorimotor Period when he constructed the scheme of the permanent object. It gives a stability to his world that it has never had before.

----

*It is not until he enters the Period of Formal Operations, at around eleven or twelve years of age, that he is able to conserve volume. That is, if you immerse that now-familiar plasticene pair, the ball and the sausage, in equal amounts of water held in twin beakers, he can tell by the level of the water that the two immersed objects are equal. This achievement apparently awaits the development of an integrated system of spatial coordinates such that a part of a given volume can be "used up" by an object, so that any material that had previously occupied that space must be displaced by an amount equal to the volume of the object. That requires a somewhat more complicated cognitive structure than knowing that a piece of plasticene is the same size when it is altered in shape.

CONSERVATION OF NUMBER

The problem we shall put to our subject in this section was devised as a test of an ability called *conservation of numerical correspondence*. The term "conservation" here refers to the child's realization that the number of objects in a display remains the same in spite of the extension of those objects in space. The subject is presented with several vases arranged in a neat row and a larger number of flowers in a bunch. He is asked to arrange the flowers "one flower for each vase, as many vases as flowers."[9]

Preoperational

Early in the Preoperational Period, the child cannot even arrange the flowers in a one-to-one relation with the vases. He may set up two lines of equal length, and then be surprised if they don't come out even when he actually places the flowers into the vases.

Later, when he is able to establish the one-to-one correspondence by himself, he can easily be fooled if the experimenter arranges one set of objects (the vases) in a line and the other set (the flowers) in a cluster; he no longer perceives the number of flowers to be equal to that of the vases, even if each flower is taken directly from a vase just before the rearrangement.

In terms of the "limitations of the Preoperational child" listed on page 69, this performance would seem to involve at least *centering, states vs. transformation, irreversibility,* and *transductive reasoning*. And all of those may be conceived in terms of classes-and-relations structure (see Fig. 4.11). The row of flowers can

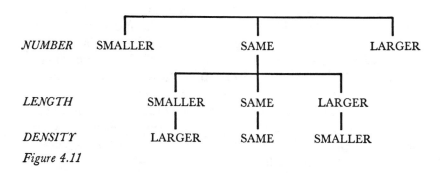

Figure 4.11

be classified as smaller than, the same as, or larger than the row of vases. But that can be done on any of three dimensions: number, length, or density. Apparently what happens is that the subject fastens upon the length dimension of the row of flowers (*centering, states vs. transformation*) and fails to return to the representation of "same number" (*irreversibility, transductive reasoning*).

The child of this age lacks the classes-and-relations structure; and until he has that, those "limitations" will recur.

Concrete Operations

In the Concrete Operations Period, however, there is never any question about the outcome. The child not only arranges the display correctly but is certain that he is correct, and he cannot be fooled when the experimenter arranges one of the sets into a cluster. When asked why he answers as he does, he says something like "They came out of the vases, so they'll go back into them." "These are stretched out more, but there's just as many of those." The *decentering* and *reversal* processes are effective, and the equivalence of the sets is permanent.

NUMBERING

According to Piaget, numbering is a synthesis of two other operations: *classification* and *seriation*.

Cardination is one aspect of classification; it determines the extension of a class; i.e., it answers the question, "How many?" The objects within a class are treated as equal with respect to that class. But in order to ascertain the extension "5," for example, one must arrange the objects in a series (they must be placed in order: this one is 1, that one 2, and so on until the supply is exhausted—a process called *ordination* or "seriation"), and the members of a series can*not* be equal. Numerical units are therefore all *different* from each other during an operation that results in the formation of a class of *identical* elements.

Furthermore, the child does not really understand numbering until he can synthesize these two into a single reversible operation. "Reversible" here means that he can move back and forth from cardination to ordination.

Let's see how these conceptions apply to Piaget's "dolls-and-sticks problem." Here the child is presented with 10 dolls that differ greatly in height and 10 sticks that also vary in length, but less so than the dolls do. He is told that the dolls are going for a walk and is asked to arrange the dolls and sticks "so that each doll can easily find the stick that belongs to it." If he succeeds in this, it will be by placing the two series parallel to each other, each in serial order of size, as indicated in Figure 4.12. But then

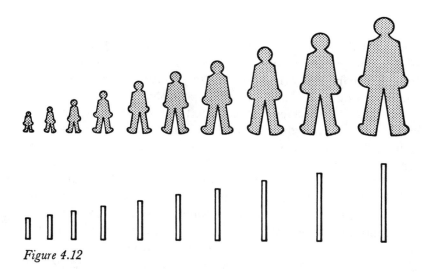

Figure 4.12

the experimenter spreads the sticks apart, so that corresponding elements of the two series are no longer opposite each other, points to one of the dolls, and asks, "Which stick will this one take?"[10]

Preoperational

In the early part of the Preoperational Period, the child fails to make even the semblance of a correct response to this problem. He fails to match the two series because he cannot arrange either one by itself into the proper order, and he cannot arrange any series in order because he lacks the structure by virtue of which any two relations $A > B$ and $B > C$ may be joined into a superordinate relation $A > C$. (See Fig. 4.13.) This property of

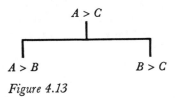

Figure 4.13

transitivity is essential to any serializing operation. Without it, he has no compunction about placing B before A in the series if he happens to be centering on the B-C relation at the time, and the matching of sticks to dolls is impossible.

Later in the Preoperational Period, the child can construct a series if given enough time, and he can match the sticks to the dolls if both are arranged in the same order; but if the two series are reversed—so that in one the units get bigger from left to right, but in the other from right to left—he fails again.

What he frequently does with the reversed series is to count; but when he "counts," all he is doing is pointing to one object after another while saying numbers that he has been taught to say in a given order. That is not true numbering, because the child has not yet achieved a synthesis of ordination and cardination.

Lacking that synthesis, the Preoperational child will often select the large (or small) end of each series as a starting point, mechanically count the dolls up to, but not including, the reference doll, and then count the same distance from the end of the series of sticks (see Fig. 4.14). His mental activity is probably something like this: he *classifies* three dolls as smaller than the reference doll (remember that the members of a class are all alike); then he counts the members of that class; and finally he applies the resulting *cardinal* number to the stick *series*, with only a fleeting reference to order as he locates the starting point.

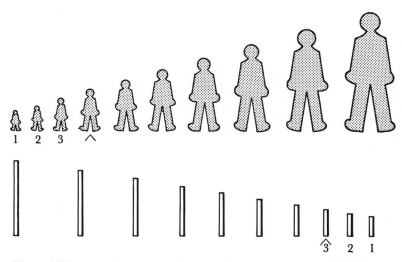

Figure 4.14

He can arrange the objects in order of size, but when he does so, he ignores their number; and he can count, but when he does so, he ignores differences in size.

Concrete Operations

It is not until he reaches the Concrete Operations Period that he is able to put the two together. Now he can select the matching stick for any specified doll, even when one series is the reverse of the other, because cardination and ordination are for him parts of a single system.[11]

EGOCENTRISM IN THE REPRESENTATION OF OBJECTS

As was noted in Chapter III, the Preoperational child has a well-developed representational ability. But there are still significant limitations on that ability. One such limitation is the inability to imagine an object from the perspective of another person. Piaget and Inhelder[12] have devised a simple test of this called the three-mountain problem (see Fig. 4.15)[13]. They set three "mountains" on a table and one chair at each side of the

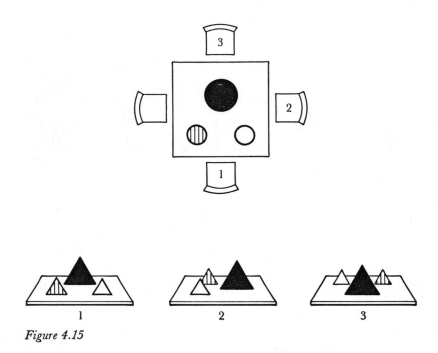

Figure 4.15

table. The child sits in one of the chairs, and a doll is moved from one to another of the three remaining chairs. Then the subject is asked what the doll sees from each of its three stations. He may respond by drawing a doll's-eye view from each position, by selecting from drawings already made, or by constructing the doll's view with cardboard cut-outs.

Preoperational

The Preoperational child simply cannot do this at all.

Concrete Operations

In the early part of the Concrete Operations Period, some transformations are made correctly, but performance is extremely erratic. It is only in the latter half of the period that the child can identify the doll's view with confidence and accuracy.

EGOCENTRISM IN SOCIAL RELATIONS

Related to the child's ability to take another person's point of view toward a physical display are certain naturalistic observations of children in social situations—notably, situations in which they interact with each other.

Preoperational

There is a strong tendency, in such situations, for children in the Preoperational period to engage either in *simple monologues*, which conform to the content of their own individual activities, or in *collective monologues*, in which Child A says something to Child B with no apparent intent that Child B should reply, or even hear; whereupon Child B does not, in fact, give any indication that he has heard, and responds by saying something totally unrelated to what Child A has just said.

They are incapable of intercommunication because neither of them is capable of taking the role of the other.

Concrete Operations

The development of concrete operations, with its increased mobility of thought, permits the child to shift rapidly back and forth between his own viewpoint and that of the other person.

It also makes possible the sharing of goals and the recognition of mutual responsibilities in the attainment of shared goals. In short, it makes cooperation possible.

"Cooperation" is "co-operation"—i.e., a coordination of operations. It is at about this time (age seven) that children begin to be interested in games with rules. In order to play such a game, one must be able to conceptualize the roles of the other players, and in fact children do develop this interest at the very same time that they begin to show in other ways their emancipation from egocentricity.*

---

*They find it difficult, however, to empathize with any younger child who spoils their game because he lacks this ability to conceptualize the interrelationship of roles.

EGOCENTRISM IN REASONING

Social interaction, however, has implications beyond itself—notably in the development of logical reasoning. For "reasoning is always a demonstration,"[14] and until the child is aware of a *need* for demonstration, he makes little progress toward developing that ability. Merely interacting freely with his physical environment results in some awareness of gaps and inconsistencies in his thinking, but what really brings them into focus is the difficulties that arise when he attempts to communicate his thoughts to others.

Piaget has done a series of studies on judgement and reasoning. One kind of study consists of a careful observation of children's spontaneous talking; another sets some task for them and then observes their reactions. Results from both kinds of study are essentially the same.

An interesting investigation of the latter kind concerns the conjunction "because." There are three modal uses of "because" that are legitimate expressions of relations between adjacent clauses:

1. *Causal explanation* establishes a cause-and-effect relation between two facts. ("He slipped because the pavement was icy.")

2. *Psychological* (or "motivational") explanation establishes a cause-and-effect relation between an intention and an act. ("I hit him because he took my candy." In this case, the intention is implied. Taking candy is not the proximate cause of being hit; anger and aggressive intent intervene.)

3. *Logical implication* establishes a reason-and-consequence relation between two ideas or two judgments. ("[I know] that animal is not dead because it is still moving.")[15]

Preoperational

The young child fails to discriminate among the three kinds of relations. In fact, within the causal mode, he often cannot even discriminate between a cause and its effect. Here are some responses to uncompleted sentences:

> I've lost my pen because *I'm not writing*.
>
> The man fell from his bicycle because *he broke his arm*.
>
> I teased that dog because *he bit me*.[16]

The "because" in each of these cases could be replaced by "and" or "in such a manner that." It is not a causal, a logical, or even a psychological relation; rather, it is a "consecutive" relation. The child does not use it consistently, however, even in that way; instead, he employs consecutive narrations, causal and psychological explanations, and even logical implications indiscriminately.* He has a foggy impression that two clauses belong together, and he uses "because" to make the connection; but he does not concern himself with the question of what *kind* of a relationship it is. His thinking consists of a mere *juxtaposition* of facts or ideas.

He really doesn't care about such distinctions, for in his egocentrism he believes that everyone thinks just as he does and therefore that he will be perfectly understood when he expresses his thoughts. He will experience many attempted communications between himself and others before that belief will change.

---

*In a more free-form situation than the incomplete-sentence task, the confusions between causal and psychological explanations are so frequent that Piaget has found it useful to classify them into subcategories. One such category is *animism*—so called because the child imputes life to inanimate objects. In one demonstration, for example, he hung a metal box by two strings that were twisted in such a way that they would rotate the box as its weight pulled them out straight. The box was then released, and the subject was questioned about its spinning. The following dialogue is eloquent testimony to the young child's tendency to give psychological explanations of physical events:

Why does it turn? *Because the string is twisted.*
Why does the string turn too? *Because it wants to unwind itself.*
Does the string know it is twisted? *Yes.*
Why? *Because it wants to untwist itself. It knows it's twisted.*[17]

Concrete Operations

It seems paradoxical that egocentrism is overcome by becoming self-conscious, but that's the way it happens. Even as sensori-motor egocentrism was overcome when the infant became aware of himself as an object among other objects, so the older child has overcome his egocentrism when he can see himself as a thinker among other thinkers. And even as that change in the sensori-motor infant comes about as a result of interaction with those other objects, so the analogous change occurs in the older child as a result of interaction with those other thinkers.

By the age of seven or eight, the average child makes a distinction between psychological and causal explanations; but he still has trouble with logical implication and often reverts to psychological explanation in its stead. ("Half of 6 is 3 because *it's right*."[18] Eventually, at about the age of nine, he produces a full-fledged logical justification. ("Half of 6 is 3 because 3 plus 3 is 6.")

That performance is possible because the child is now capable of imposing direction and order on his thinking—a direction and order that he has found useful in communicating with others. "Only by means of friction against other minds," says Piaget, "by means of exchange and opposition does thought come to be conscious of its own aims and tendencies, and only in this way is it obliged to relate what could till then remain juxtaposed."[19]

ESTIMATING WATER LINES

We have seen (Chapter 1, p. 10) that even the simplest of object perceptions is built up over a long period of time. It should not be surprising to find that development of an extensive system of spatial coordinates takes even longer.

It shouldn't be, but it is! Here is a demonstration: a child is presented with a glass bottle one-fourth filled with colored water and another (or an outline drawing thereof) just like it but without the water. The second bottle is tipped off the vertical and the subject is asked to indicate where its waterline would be if the water from the first bottle were poured into it.[20]

Preoperational

In the latter part of the Preoperational Period, the child centers on the configuration of the bottle, and the waterline is drawn with reference to that only (Fig. 4.16).

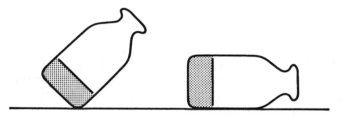

Figure 4.16

Concrete Operations

The early part of the Concrete Operations Period is a transitional stage in which there is a conflict between taking reference cues from the bottle and using the more stable horizontal and vertical contours of the surround (Fig. 4.17). It is not until the

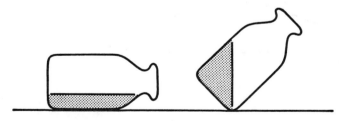

Figure 4.17

child is nine or ten years old that he is able to give the correct response consistently (Fig. 4.18).

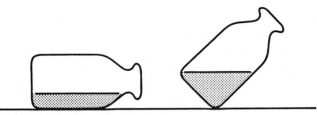

Figure 4.18

To me, the striking thing about all this is that the Euclidean space that we all take for granted not only is constructed rather than given, but is constructed over a period that covers most of a person's growing years.

DISTANCE, TIME, MOVEMENT, AND VELOCITY

Another such construction is that of *time*.[21] Children's answers to questions about time are often mildly surprising to adults, but when observations are made in situations deliberately contrived to illuminate the salient features of their thinking, the results are sometimes downright astonishing!

If the experimenter moves one object (*A*) from *a* to *d* and simultaneously moves another object (*B*) from *a* to *b* (Fig. 4.19),

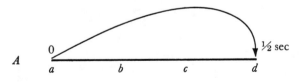

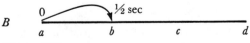

Figure 4.19

the early Preoperational child will insist that A "took longer" than B. Even more surprising is his response when the B object is moved twice (Fig. 4.20). The child may still maintain that A took longer than B!

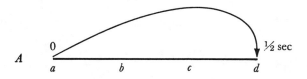

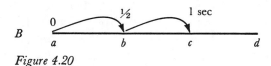

Figure 4.20

He may say that A took longer because it is ahead of B or that B took a shorter time because it didn't have so far to go. In either case, he is centering on the spatial characteristics of the event and more particularly on spatial *states* (as opposed to transformations); whereas movement (distance), velocity, and time in an adult are all differentiated parts of a single cognitive structure. That structure begins to form in the Preoperational Period, but it is thoroughly dominated by spatial perceptions.

In order to have a conception of time, it is necessary to develop conceptions of movement and velocity. But in order to have a conception of velocity, for example, it is necessary to develop a conception of time. It looks like a vicious circle; but before we give up, let's take a closer look at the child's conception of velocity.

Velocity is a relation between time and movement. We have seen how the young child deals with time; now let's test his conception of movement—i.e., the spatial displacement of an object in his visual field. The child is told that the two lines in Figure 4.21 are streetcar tracks, and that any small object moved along it is a streetcar. The experimenter moves a "car" over a given

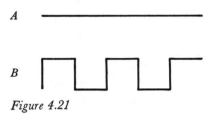

Figure 4.21

number of segments of Track *B* and asks the child to make a trip of the same length on *A* with his car. Since the movement is over a *distance*, this is a test of the *conservation of length* (distance).*

The child probably will move his car to a position opposite that of the experimenter, which of course means that his trip has actually been less than half as long. The early Preoperational child will continue to respond in this way even when supplied with a piece of cardboard—a potential measuring device—exactly equal in length to a segment of Track *B*.

This performance seems to have one characteristic in common with that of the time problem presented earlier. In both, there apparently is a centering on terminal spatial order—i.e., given simultaneous starts from identical points on the spatial dimension "left-to-right," the child's answer depends on which car is farther to the right at the end of the episode.

We suspect, then, that centering on terminal position is at least a part of the problem—a hypothesis that can be applied to *velocity* problems.

---

*The most common method of testing for conservation of length is to display horizontally two sticks that the child recognizes as the same length, then to move one of them slightly to the right and ask him whether they are still the same length.

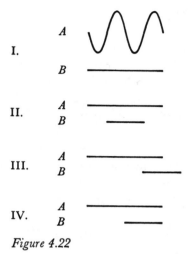

I. A

    B

II. A

    B

III. A

     B

IV. A

    B

Figure 4.22

In Figure 4.22, *A* represents the route of one object, *B* that of another; the Roman numerals indicate different problems, each of which takes but a few seconds to administer. In each of the four problems, the two objects start simultaneously and stop simultaneously. It is therefore obvious to an adult that in each problem, the velocity of Object *A* is greater than that of Object *B*.

But here are the responses of a subject in the Preoperational Subperiod:

In problem I the child says that "*A* and *B* travel at the same speed," which they don't.

In problem II, he says that "*A* is faster than *B*," which, of course, is correct.

In problem III, he says that "*B* is faster than *A*," which it is not.

In problem IV, he believes that "*A* is faster," which, like his response to problem II, is correct.

Thus II and IV are correct; I and III are not, since A is in fact faster than B in all four problems.

However, the interesting question in each case is, "Why?" All but one of those performances confirm the "terminal position" hypothesis. In I, II, and III, terminal position and perceived speed agree precisely, whereas in IV the hypothesis calls for a "same speed" response, and that is not what happens.

A slight variation in the experimental procedure gives us a clue to the reason for that exception. In this version of problem IV, the objects move through tunnels from their initial to their final positions. When that is done, the child does say that they move at the same speed; and that, of course, is in line with the "terminal position" hypothesis.

But why should the addition of the tunnel have such an effect? Apparently there is another structure, "the passing schema," that dominates over terminal position when the two are in conflict. The "passing schema" is activated whenever one object is seen to overtake another (even if the action stops before an actual passing occurs). What the tunnel does is to prevent that structure from operating, so that the child then falls back onto his terminal position scheme.

Thus, although centering on terminal position is not what determines the response in all of the examples we have discussed here, there does seem to be a kind of centering that limits the competence of the Preoperational child in each one; and with the single exception of the "passing schema," that centering is on an end state rather than a transformation.

Shifting back to time for a moment, we find centering again when we ask a young child how old someone is compared to someone else. His reply will depend entirely upon the heights of the two persons judged. It might be regarded as a sort of "vertical terminal position" effect!

On page 113, we encountered a vicious circle in which the development of each of three concepts,

time $(t = d/v)$,
movement $(d = vt)$,
velocity $(v = d/t)$,

is dependent on the development of each of the others. Have we broken out of that circle? I'm not sure that we have. As a matter of fact, the physicists themselves have had trouble with this one, though Piaget suggests that a breakthrough may be in the making. A French physicist has proposed that velocity be defined in terms of the notion of passing—which is precisely the way in which the Preoperational child "defines" it![22]

SUMMARY

Since birth, the dominant mental activities of the child have changed from *overt actions* (in the Sensorimotor Period) to *perceptions* (in the Preoperational Period) to *intellectual operations* (in the Concrete Operations Period). Those operations occur within a framework of classes and relations that make possible what Piaget calls *mobility* of thinking—decentering, reversibility, taking the view of others, etc. As a result, the Concrete Operational child conserves quantity and number, constructs the time and space that he will live with as an adult, and establishes foundations for the kind of thinking that is the identifying feature of the next and final period of his intellectual development, Formal Operations.

NOTES

[1] Jean Piaget and Bärbel Inhelder, *The Child's Conception of Space*, trans. F. J. Langdon and J. L. Lunzer (London: Routledge & Kegan Paul Ltd.), 1956, p. 36.

[2] John H. Flavell, *The Developmental Psychology of Jean Piaget* (Princeton: D. Van Nostrand Co., Inc.), 1963, p. 166.

[3] "The Theory of Stages in Cognitive Development," *in* Donald R. Green, Marguerite P. Ford, and Gerald B. Flamer (eds.) *Measurement and Piaget* (New York: McGraw-Hill Book Co.), 1971, p. 2.

[4] Flavell, *The Developmental Psychology of Jean Piaget*, p. 166.

[5] This discussion leans heavily on the synthesizing work of Flavell, *Ibid.*, pp. 168ff.

[6] The primary source of the material in this section is Jean Piaget and Bärbel Inhelder, *La Genese des Structures Logiques Elementaire: Classifications et Seriations*, 1959; the recommended reference in English is Flavell, *The Developmental Psychology of Jean Piaget*.

[7] This is similar to a problem first described in Jean Piaget and Alina Szeminska, *The Child's Conception of Number*, trans. C. Cattengo and F. M. Hodgson (New York: Humanities Press), 1952, p. 165. The quotations are paraphrased.

[8] Piaget and Inhelder, *La Genese des Structures Logiques Elementaire*, 1959, pp. 55–56; as quoted by Flavell in his *The Developmental Psychology of Jean Piaget*.

[9] Piaget and Szeminska, *The Child's Conception of Number*, p. 49.

[10] *Ibid.*, p. 97.

[11] *Ibid.*, pp. 147–157.

[12] Piaget and Inhelder, *The Child's Conception of Space*, p. 210.

[13] Adapted from Piaget and Inhelder, *The Child's Conception of Space*, p. 211.

[14] Jean Piaget, *Judgement and Reasoning in the Child*, trans. Marjorie Worden (New York: Harcourt, Brace & World, Inc.), 1928, p. 2.

[15] *Ibid.*, p. 6.

[16] *Ibid.*, p. 17.

[17] Jean Piaget, *The Child's Conception of the World*, trans. Jean and Andrew Tomlinson (New York: Harcourt, Brace & World, Inc.), 1930.

[18] Piaget, *Judgement and Reasoning in the Child*, p. 26.

[19] *Ibid.*, pp. 11–12.

[20] Adapted from Piaget and Inhelder, *The Child's Conception of Space*, p. 383.

[21] A more detailed account of the experiments on time, measurement, and velocity is available in Chapter 9 of Flavell's *The Developmental Psychology of Jean Piaget, 1963*. See especially pp. 316–326.

[22] Jean Piaget, "The Child and Modern Physics," *Scientific American*, vol. 196 (March 1957), p. 51.

5

Formal Operations Period
(11-15 years)

5

Formal Operations Period

Marvelous though they are when compared, for example, to the most advanced thinking of any subhuman species, Concrete Operations still fall far short of the intellectual accomplishments of an intelligent human adult. My purpose in this chapter is not to analyze those adult accomplishments in great detail, but rather to identify the crucial characteristics that differentiate them from earlier ones. Consequently, the chapter is relatively brief.

Another reason for the relative brevity of this chapter is that the characteristics of adult thinking are somewhat more accessible than are the processes discussed earlier. Every college course is an enterprise that requires a great deal of thinking; hopefully, much of it is logical. One who is looking for the *operations* involved in that thinking may be able to find some of them. A better way to focus attention on those operations would be to take a course in logic. Those students who can arrange to include such a course in their curriculum should do so, but should look at it from a psychological viewpoint, remembering always the Piagetian dictum that *logic* is the mirror of *thought*, rather than vice versa. That is, the function of logic is to make explicit those mental processes that occur naturally at the highest level of human development.

Before turning the reader over to a logician, however, there are a few general things that I wish to say about the transition from Concrete to Formal Operations. I shall describe but a single problem, so that its implications may be examined in reasonable detail.

ARCHIMEDES' LAW OF FLOATING BODIES

An object will float if its specific gravity is less than 1.00—i.e., if its density is less than that of water. In an experimental test, this can be reduced to a comparison of the *weights of equal volumes* of the two substances. Some subjects are able to derive this law while being questioned by the investigator. But by no means are all of them competent to do so, and the differences among them are related to differences in age.

> *Apparatus*
> The subject is presented with
>   1) a bucket of water,
>   2) several different objects, each small enough to fit into the bucket, and
>   3) an empty plastic cube to facilitate comparisons of the density of the objects with the density of water.

> *Procedure*
> The subject is asked to classify the objects according to whether they will float and to explain the basis of his classification in each case. Then he is allowed to experiment with the materials and is asked to summarize his observations and to look for a *law* that will tie them all together.

CONCRETE OPERATIONS APPLIED TO
THE FLOATING BODIES PROBLEM

My purpose in this and the following two sections (*Operations on Operations* and *The Real versus the Possible*) is to analyze the behavior of school-age children and adolescents in the situation described above. I shall first present some examples of performances by subjects who are not yet in the Formal Operations Period.

Although the Preoperational child in this situation blithely invokes a special cause for each event, the Concrete Operational child is troubled by inconsistencies that had not concerned him earlier because they had not existed for him; he had lacked "instruments of coordination (operational classifications, etc.), which will attain equilibrium only at the point when concrete operations are structured."[1]

That equilibrium is not attained suddenly, but progress is made precisely because of the child's awareness that he is in difficulty. In the early part of the Concrete Operations Period, the main contradiction is that certain large objects will float and certain small ones sink. It is a contradiction because he begins the period with a kind of "absolute weight" concept as his main tool for dealing with the problem. Each object, including each bucket of water, has a "weight" that is conceived as a force that somehow opposes other forces, but in no consistent manner. (Remember that weight is not yet being conserved.) One moment he may predict that water will push a solid object up, the next moment that it will push one down. Initially, the only "weight" he knows is a property of each separate object, not of the substance of which the object is constituted; hence the term "absolute weight." Moreover, the child assigns a weight to an object by placing it on a scale something like that shown in

SMALL, LIGHT   *TO*   LARGE, HEAVY

Figure 5.1

Figure 5.1; size and weight are not discriminated as separate dimensions. That soon changes, however.

> BAR [seven years, eleven months] first classifies the bodies into three categories: those that float because they are light [wood, matches, paper, and the aluminum cover]; those that sink because they are heavy [large and small keys, pebbles of all sizes, ring clamps, needles and nails, a metal cylinder, and an eraser]; and those that remain suspended at a midway point [fish].
> "The needle?"
> "It goes down because it's iron."
> "And the key?"
> "It sinks too."
> "And the small things?" [nails, ring clamps].
> "They are iron too."
> "And this little pebble?"
> "It's heavy because it's stone."
> "And the little nail?"
> "It's just a little heavy."
> "And the cover, why does it stay up?"
> "It has edges and sinks if it's filled with water."
> "Why?"
> "Because it's iron."[2]

One process that seems to be going on here is the assimilation of new objects into established categories. The needle "goes down because it's iron"; the nails, ring clamps, and probably the key "are iron too." The pebble is "heavy because it's stone." Even the aluminum pan lid, which does not sink unless it is filled with water, is said to sink "because it's iron." The classification of some substances as light and others as heavy is a step toward the conception of density—i.e., the classification of substances according to their weights with volume held constant. That this child can*not* conceive density should not be surprising if you remember that neither of its two ingredients—weight and volume—is yet being conserved.

Although it does not always show in the protocols, children early in the Concrete Operations period often make a three-way "sinkability" classification. Some objects can be relied upon to float, others will surely sink, and still others may either float or sink, depending on the circumstances (e.g., the aluminum pan lid mentioned above).

The foregoing example (BAR, age seven years, eleven months) demonstrates the Concrete Operational child's ability to classify objects; but it also reveals a notable lack of refinement of the relevant structures. What the child needs as a foundation for the impending "operations on operations" stage is a structure something like that shown in Figure 5.2, which relates the perceived

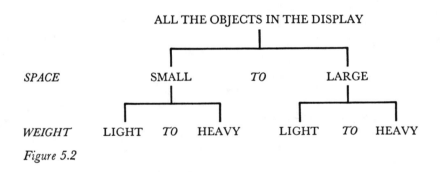

Figure 5.2

space occupied by a body to its perceived weight. Does he have such a structure? Here is BAR again, thirteen months later:

> BAR (nine years). [Class 1] Floating objects; ball, pieces of wood, corks, and an aluminum plate. [Class 2] Sinking objects: keys, metal weights, needles, stones, large block of wood, and a piece of wax. [Class 3] Objects that may either float or sink: covers. [Seeing] a needle at the bottom of the water [BAR] says:
> "Ah! They are too heavy for the water, so the water can't carry them."
> "And the tokens?"
> "I don't know; they are more likely to go under."
> "Why do these things float?" [Class 1]
> "Because they are quite light."
> "And the covers?"

"They can go to the bottom because the water can come up over the top."
"And why do these things sink?" [Class 2]
"Because they are heavy."
"The big block of wood?"
"It will go under."
"Why?"
"There is too much water for it to stay up."
"And the needles?"
"They are lighter."
"So?"
"If the wood were the same size as the needle, it would be lighter."
"Put the candle in the water. Why does it stay up?"
"I don't know."
"And the cover?"
"It's iron; that's not too heavy, and there is enough water to carry it."
"And now?" [It sinks.]
"That's because the water got inside."
"And put the wooden block in."
"Ah! Because it's wood that is wide enough not to sink."
"If it were a cube?"
"I think that it would go under."
"And if you push it under?"
"I think it would come back up."
"And if you push this plate?" [aluminum]
"It would stay at the bottom."
"Why?"
"Because the water weights on the plate."
"Which is heavier, the plate or the wood?"
"The piece of wood."
"Then why does the plate stay at the bottom?"
"Because it's a little lighter than the wood; when there is water on top there is less resistance and it can stay down. The wood has resistance, and it comes back up."
"And this little piece of wood?"
"No, it will come back up because it is even lighter than the plate."
"And if we begin again with this large piece of wood in the smallest bucket, will the same thing happen?"
"No, it will come back up because the water isn't strong enough: there is not enough weight from the water [to hold down the wood]."[3]

I'm sure we can agree that BAR is pretty badly confused. He did, at one point near the beginning of the episode, hit upon an idea that might have been expanded into a solution: he said, "If the wood were the same size as the needle, it would be lighter." Why did he fail to develop that point? He failed because he still lacks the structure delineated in Figure 5.2. Instead of utilizing a general operational form in dealing with the relation of weight to occupied space, he is virtually limited to a particular case—the comparison of iron with wood. Moreover, when he does make comparisons, they are (with the single exception noted above) not comparisons of the weights of *equal amounts* of substances. The concept of specific gravity demands just such a comparison. But when BAR compares the weight of an object with that of water, he compares it with the entire quantity of water in the bucket: the same piece of wood will sink in one bucket, float in another.

Thus, bothered by vaguely perceived inadequacies in his explanations, BAR blunders energetically into one contradiction after another, until by the end of the session he has reverted to explanation by absolute weight.

It is a temporary regression, however. In general, the Concrete Operational child is much more orderly in his thinking than that. Even in the earlier session (seven years, eleven months) BAR classified the objects into three "sinkability" categories. And the third of those categories (objects that float or sink, depending on the circumstances) becomes further refined during the course of the period:

> RAY [nine years]: "The wood isn't the same as iron. It's lighter; there are holes in between." "And steel?" "It stays under because there aren't any holes in between."
> DUM [nine years, six months]: The wood floats "because there is air inside"; the key does not "because there isn't any air inside."[4]

"Float-or-sink-depending-on-the-circumstances" has become "more-or-less-filled," and that serves the child quite well in his quest for reduction of inconsistencies.

On the other hand, since "the water" is for him the volume of all the water in the container rather than just that displaced by the object, the ultimate explicit comparison between a measured volume of water and an equal volume of the other substance does not occur. Until he can understand the dynamics of displacement of liquids (i.e., until he can conserve volume) it *cannot* occur. The SPACE dimension in Figure 5.2 must be replaced by VOLUME, and the subject must realize that density varies directly with weight and inversely with volume. The revised structure is more difficult to diagram, but I have attempted it in Figure 5.3.

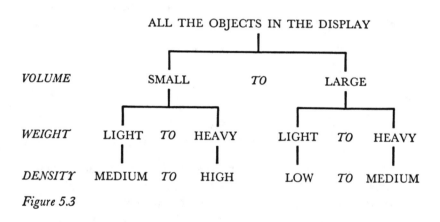

Figure 5.3

The adolescent who *has* developed that structure can think of displaced water as one of the objects in the display; all that is needed now to solve the floating-bodies problem is an explicit comparison of *equal* volumes of (1) water and (2) the substance of the target object. But since neither conservation of volume nor the elaborated structure becomes available until the Formal Operations Period, that solution is normally deferred until the subject is at least eleven years of age.

OPERATIONS ON OPERATIONS

When weight and volume do at last become operational, the adolescent can place them in a logical relationship to each other —a relation known as *proportion*:*

$$\frac{W}{V} = d,$$

where

W is the weight† of a body,
V is the volume of that body, and
d is its density.

If we assume that an object is "solid," it will float if its "specific gravity" is less than 1.00—i.e., if

$$\frac{d_0}{d_w} < 1,$$

where

d_0 is the density of the object and
d_w is the density of water.

The important thing to note about all this is that the adolescent is *operating on operations*. Piaget refers to *second-order operations*, and if my reading of him is correct, those operations constitute one of the fundamental characteristics of the Formal Operations Period.

---

*Actually, volume conservation itself involves a proportion, since as one dimension of a solid is doubled, the product of the other two must be halved. If we start with a 2-inch cube, for example, the transformation will be:

$$A_1 \times B_1 \times C_1 = A_1(B_1 \times C_1) = 2(2 \times 2) = 8 \text{ cubic inches,}$$

or

$$A_2 \times B_2 \times C_2 = A_2(B_2 \times C_2) = 4(1 \times 2) = 8 \text{ cubic inches.}$$

†A general formula would have to invoke the concept of *mass*; but in this situation, weight is satisfactory because the force of gravity remains constant from one observation to another.

A Concrete Operational child knows that the product of replicating a given object 3 times is 3 (not counting the model, of course), and he knows that if that set of 3 is replicated 4 times, he'll have 12 of the objects. The adolescent has mastered those operations, but he can also place the resulting sets into relationship to each other: 12 is to 3 as 4 is to 1. To put it another way, 12/3 has the same *form* as 4/1. Before he can understand such a relationship, the adolescent must be able to *operate* formally *on* concrete *operations*.

In the Piagetian experiments, the concept of weight involves at least the operations of placing an object in a *series* of small to large gravity forces and of establishing a *correspondence* between that series and a series of inputs from the balance scale used to measure it. Moreover, the concept of volume requires similar, though more complex, operations, including the structuring of a correspondence between visual space and displacement of liquid. Those are operations with objects, and they are necessasy to the solution of the floating-bodies problem. They are *necessary*, but not *sufficient*. The adolescent starts with concrete operations; but then, in the floating-bodies problem, he places them into a logical relationship to each other—a proportion ($W/V = d$). Indeed, in order to educe the concept of "specific gravity," he must make a proportion out of two other proportions (W_0/V_0 and W_w/V_w). In each case, he *operates on operations*.

THE REAL VERSUS THE POSSIBLE

As he grows older and gains more experience, the child's construction of reality becomes more precise and extended, and that makes him aware of gaps in his understanding that had been masked by the vagueness of his previous constructions. He fills those gaps with *hypotheses*, and he is able to formulate—and often even to test—hypotheses without actually manipulating concrete objects. More accurately, he develops a new theoretical synthesis in which "certain relations are necessary,"[5] so that particular propositions can be checked, not only against the data of his senses (and against the data-bound mental operations of the previous period) but also against this new structure of *possibilities*. In fact, he *begins* by considering possibilities.

The following examples illustrate formal operations in the floating bodies problem:

> FRAN [twelve years, one month] does not manage to discover the law, but neither does he accept any of the earlier hypotheses. He classifies correctly the objects presented here but hesitates before the aluminum wire.
> "Why are you hesitating?"
> "Because of the lightness, but no, that has no effect."
> "Why?"
> "The lightness has no effect. It depends on the sort of matter: for example, the wood can be heavy, and it floats." And for the cover: "I thought of the surface."
> "The surface plays a role?"
> "Maybe, the surface that touches the water, but that doesn't mean anything."
> Thus he discards all of his hypotheses without finding a solution.
> FIS [twelve years, six months] also . . . comes close to solution, saying in reference to a penny that it sinks "because it is small, it isn't stretched enough. . . . You would have to have something larger to stay at the surface, something of the same weight and which would have a greater extension."[6]

Observe the difference between these performances and those of the Concrete Operational child. Here there is a kind of transcendence of the immediate—a systematic trying out of possibilities. These subjects actually formulate hypotheses about the problem.

A child in the Concrete Operations Period does not formulate hypotheses, in the usual sense of imagining what events would occur under conditions that also are imagined. His accommodations are to events in the real world; he can only classify objects or events, place them in serial relationship to each other, and establish a correspondence of units in different categories. Tall dolls get tall sticks; greater movement of a spring balance means heavier weight; certain materials sink while others float; and so on. It is true that the ability to do these things implies a cognitive framework into which yet-to-be-experienced events can be placed (e.g., if he has built a structure in which $A<B<C$, he can extend the series to D, E, F, etc., or if $A < C < E$, he may interpolate B and D); but the possible is always a limited and direct extension of concrete reality.

At the age of twelve, however, we find FRAN trying out *hypotheses* in his mind and discarding them as inappropriate, without any necessity of actually manipulating materials. FIS transforms the "more-or-less-filled" category of the Concrete Operations Period into a relationship between the weight-to-volume ratio of the object and the weight-to-volume ratio of water. And at age fourteen, another subject (WYR) actually manipulates one variable systematically while holding all others constant, which of course is the classical method of experimental science; but the experiments are designed to provide empirical tests of *possibilities* conceived *before* any manipulation.

The Preoperational child is capable of preposterous flights of fancy; the Concrete Operational child's thinking is limited by his concern for organizing the actual data of his senses. The adolescent in the Period of Formal Operations is like both of those and different from each. He is capable of departures from reality, but those departures are lawful; he is concerned with reality, but reality is only a subset within a much larger set of possibilities.

EGOCENTRISM

The introduction to "possibilities" has a curious side effect. The subject's thinking becomes *egocentric*. The term "egocentrism" is usually used by Piagetian scholars to refer to one outstanding characteristic of a child's thinking while he is in the Preoperational Period. In truth, however, Piaget says that egocentrism occurs not in just one period but in each of three periods.

The three major periods of development—Sensorimotor, Concrete Operations, and Formal Operations*—represent three different fields of cognitive action, and at the beginning of each there is a relative lack of structural differentiation and functional equilibrium. To the neonate, the world is *his actions* upon it; to the Preoperational child, his *representations* of the world of physical objects are the only ones possible. The adolescent's egocentrism results from the extension of his thinking into the realm of the *possible* through the instruments of propositional logic. He fails "to distinguish between the ego's new and unpredicted capacities and the social or cosmic universe to which they are applied."[7] He goes through a phase during which his own cerebration seems to him omnipotent, and it is then that he is likely to annoy his elders with all sorts of idealistic schemes designed to bring reality into line with his own thinking. "The theories used to represent the world center on the role of the reformer that the adolescent feels himself called upon to play in the future."[8] He, too, is "egocentric."

"FORMAL" AS PERTAINING TO "FORM"

You should now be in a position to appreciate the significance of the title "Formal Operations." An example is the quantitative relationship cited earlier: "12 is to 3 as 4 is to 1." So too are the comprehension and appreciation of metaphor, of irony and satire, of proverbs and parables, of analogies of all kinds. Advanced mathematics and scientific constructs in many content areas are all results of formal thinking.

The adolescent can follow the form of an argument even if it means disregarding certain implications of its specific content. Younger children are not able to do that. If, for example,

---

*The Preoperational Period may be regarded as a preparation for Concrete Operations.

we present to a Concrete Operational child the following sentence:

> "I am very glad I do not (like) onions, for if I liked them, I would always be eating them, and I hate eating unpleasant things,"

he will respond to the *content* of the sentence by saying, in effect:

> "Onions are unpleasant;"
> "it is wrong not to like them"; and so on.

The adolescent, on the other hand, will respond to the *form* of the argument by focusing on the contradiction between

> "if I liked them" and
> "onions are unpleasant."[9]

Or take the syllogism

> "All children like spinach;
> boys are children;
> therefore boys like spinach."

The younger child will respond to the content (particularly if he is a boy who doesn't like spinach!), but the adolescent can follow the argument* because he is impressed by its form.

---

*He can, but that doesn't mean that he necessarily does. Morgan and Morton (*Journal of Social Psychology*, 1944) presented *college* students with the following syllogism: "Some ruthless men deserve a violent death. Since one of the most ruthless men was Heydrich, the Nazi hangman, therefore:

1. Heydrich, the Nazi hangman, deserved a violent death.
2. Heydrich may have deserved a violent death.
3. Heydrich did not deserve a violent death.
4. None of these conclusions logically follows."

Thirty-seven percent of the subjects chose number one!

Of course it is possible that those who did were still operating on a concrete level, even in college. See the report of relevant research in Chapter 6 (pp. 169–170).

SUMMARY

Let us now summarize what has been said about the Formal Operations Period. The adolescent begins where the Concrete Operational child left off—with *concrete operations*. He then *operates on those operations* by casting them into the form of propositions. The propositions then become part of a cognitive structure that owes its existence to past experience but makes possible hypotheses that do not correspond to any particular experience. The Concrete Operational child always starts with experience and makes limited interpolations and extrapolations from the data available to his senses. The adolescent, however, begins with the *possible* and then checks various possibilities against memorial representations of past experiences, and perhaps against sensory feedback from the concrete manipulations that are suggested by his hypotheses. A final reason that cognition is relatively independent of concrete reality is that the *content* of a problem has at last been subordinated to the *form* of relations within it.

All of this has consequences for education, because the content of a student's thought now is not raw data but statements about those data. He can deal at the outset with possibilities, and he can combine those to produce *implications* that are not present in the original data. And that, in turn, opens avenues of communication with the great minds of his culture.

Those and other consequences of cognitive development for education, not only at the formal level but also much earlier, constitute the substance of discussion in the next and final chapter of this book.

Now is the time for a review of Chapter 1.
See explanation in Preface to the First Edition (p. xv).

NOTES

[1]Bärbel Inhelder and Jean Piaget, *The Growth of Logical Thinking from Childhood to Adolescence*, trans. Anne Parson and S. Milgram (New York, Basic Books, Inc., 1958), p. 28.

[2]*Ibid.*, p. 29.

[3]*Ibid.*, p. 33.

[4]*Ibid.*, p. 35.

[5]*Ibid.*, p. 251.

[6]*Ibid.*, pp. 37–38.

[7]*Ibid.*, p. 345.

[8]Jean Piaget, *The Psychology of Intelligence* (London: Routledge and Kegan-Paul), 1950.

[9]The example is a nonsense-sentence by Ballard, quoted in J. McV. Hunt, *Intelligence and Experience* (New York: Ronald Press Co.), 1961, p. 232. The first line of the Hunt quotation of Ballard actually reads, "I am very glad I do not *eat* onions, . . ." [italics mine]. Since I was unable to find the original, I hope both the reader and Dr. Hunt will forgive the substitute of "like" for "eat." I am reasonably certain that the latter is an error of transcription.

6

Educational Implications: An Epilogue

6

Educational Implications: An Epilogue

When Piaget began his study of genetic epistemology about fifty years ago, probably the farthest thing from his mind was its "educational implications." He was concerned with how cognitions develop, not with developing cognitions. His writings are not addressed to educators—or even to psychologists, for that matter. He is an interdisciplinary thinker, and his main concerns are still, much as they were in the beginning, theoretical rather than practical. Although he has occasionally commented on educational practices (as virtually everyone has, in his own way), to my knowledge he has never touted his theory as the basis of a new pedagogy.

All that is entirely fitting, as far as it goes. But after all, Piaget has said some pretty important things about children, and anyone who says important things about children ultimately must be important to educators. Teaching is the manipulation of the student's environment in such a way that his activities will contribute to his development (toward goals whose definitions are not our present concern). It should be obvious to the reader by now that the effect of a given environment on a child is as much a function of the child as of the environment. If a teacher knows that, his behavior will be affected by his conception of what students are like. Indeed, his very definition of teaching will be so determined. Mine was.

In this chapter, I shall present some principles and some practices. The practices were not derived directly from the principles, but both were derived from Piaget's theory. The principles are designed to organize one's thinking about the implications of the theory. I consider here implications for two professions in education—teaching and testing.

TEACHING: PRINCIPLES

Piaget has not constructed a theory of teaching; that much is clear. But the theory is about intellectual development, and since most teaching has a similar concern, there should be some overlap between the two. Is there? Granted that the theory does not say anything about interventions as such, does it say anything that is pertinent to the concerns of those who would intervene in child development?

I believe it does. The following three principles have been derived from the theory and are stated here as laconically as possible; they are intended as reminders of some things that by this time the reader should know. Only very general prescriptions for teacher behavior are given here, but to the extent that teacher behavior is influenced by a knowledge of what goes on in the minds of students, these principles should prove helpful even without prescriptions.

CONSTRUCTION THROUGH ACTION

The mind is not a passive receptacle, but an active, organizing, dynamic system. It *constructs* the very mechanisms by which it takes in information from the environment. Every pattern of input must be run through the filter of existing structures, and at the same time every such encounter changes those structures—sometimes merely by making them more stable, but more often by effecting qualitative alterations.

Those structures are themselves the systemic properties of *actions*. At first, the actions are almost entirely overt; later, they are internalized in the form of simple representations of concrete objects and events; and, finally, they become organized into the complex networks that underlie logical thinking in the adult. From this point of view, cognition *is* action.

Another way to look at the structures of intelligence (knowledge) is to classify them according to the kinds of experience from which they emerge. Knowledge gained via logico-mathematical experience (e.g., conservation, classification, law of floating bodies) is *invented*. Knowledge gained via physical experience is *discovered* (rubber objects bounce, iron objects do not; round things roll, square ones do not; thin rods bend or break, thick ones do not). Knowledge gained through social transmission is merely *accepted* (this is a cow; we wash our hands before we eat; "he" is singular, "they" plural); but even messages of this sort must be assimilated to existing structures (e.g., the identification process in which the word "this," with or without pointing, is a signifier; the identity relation signified by "is"; the concepts referred to by each of the other words in the preceding parenthetical list), and assimilation is a process—an action. Whether the learner is a child, an adolescent, or an adult; whether the knowledge is social, physical, or logico-mathematical; a person who acquires knowledge must be active.

The Piagetian teacher discriminates among the three kinds of knowledge and differentiates his behavior accordingly. That is, he does what he can to enhance the appropriate experience in the child. If it is social knowledge, he tells the child—and models for him—what the social consensus holds to be "correct." If it is physical knowledge, he encourages the child to experiment with objects so that he might receive direct feedback from them. If it is logico-mathematical knowledge, he encourages the child to think about relationships: "Is this the same amount now as it was when it was shaped like a ball?" "Is this the same number of objects that were here before they were spread out?" "Are some of these objects alike in some way? In what way?" "If the biggest one goes here, where does the smallest belong? The ones in between?" "*Why* does this one sink and that one float?"

The mind is not a receptacle. "Teaching" is far more than "telling," and even telling—if it is to result in knowledge—must engage the listener as an active participant in the communicative process. In general, the teacher should encourage curiosity and the making of autonomous choices, for therein lie the foundations of cognitive structure.

TRANSFER AS SEQUENTIAL INTEGRATION OF STRUCTURES

All structures are built out of actions of one kind or another, but actions that produce knowledge are not aimless. They are directed and purposeful, and they always have *content*. Logical thinking, for example, is always *about* something,* and it is not possible to establish new relations unless there are some already established ideas to relate. In fact, the more ideas the child has at his disposal, the more questions are generated, and ultimately the more relations are established. Those relations are the ideas that enter into still further relations in a metastructure of increasing complexity. Taken together, they are the child's general *knowledge*, or *intelligence* (for Piaget, the two terms are synonymous); separately, they are called *structures*.

With the exception of the reflexes present at birth, structures are never "given," no matter how obvious they may seem to an adult; and unless those "obvious" structures have been constructed through experience (in a sufficiently mature organism), no amount of "training" will produce the higher levels of understanding to which educational enterprises are committed. Once basic structures have been acquired, however, they will continue

---

*There is, however, a gradual dissociation of logico-mathematical thinking from specific material content. The culmination of that trend is found in formal operations, where the content may be not objects or images of objects but "operations." (See *Operations on Operations*, pp. 128–129.)

to function intermittently through subsequent periods of development—both individually and as components of new structures.

A cognitive structure is a more or less tightly organized system of mental actions. New inputs that are congruent with an existing structure are organized by it (assimilated to it). When a child finds himself in a new situation, he thinks about it in terms of the system of mental actions that he brings to that situation. Thus, although there undoubtedly is some retention of specific "learning in the narrow sense," most effects of prior learning are effects of experience on more complex and integrated cognitive structures.

A structure (understanding, principle) then serves to organize new knowledge; conversely, the new situation may modify the structure. As indicated in the previous section, both of those events are facilitated by extensive "application" of new knowledge. But beyond that, it is important that the teacher not only recognize the child's limitations but develop a genuine appreciation for his achievements.

In this regard, some Piagetian scholars have suggested that childish thinking is not *inferior* to adult thinking, just *different*. That, in my view, is nonsense; for Piaget, development is a saltatory but inexorable progression toward the ideal of formal operations. Childish thinking, however, does have a structure of its own, and the teacher should not violate the integrity of that structure. A child who centers on length in the conservation-of-substance problem has progressed beyond the stage at which he would fail even to comprehend the question for lack of a stable notion of length *or* width. That is an achievement that should be accepted for what it is, not rejected for what it is not. His development will be enhanced if his teachers recognize his right to be wrong, for early structures are the foundations of later ones.

MOTIVATION THROUGH COGNITIVE CONFLICT

The first principle set forth here was called "construction through action"; every encounter with the real world changes cognitive structure in some way. But qualitative changes seem to depend upon the induction of a state that we shall call "cognitive conflict"—by which is meant conflict between input and cognitive structure or between structures—and upon the child's efforts to resolve that conflict and restore equilibrium.

The most feasible way to induce cognitive conflict is to arrange for optimal discrepancy between environmental inputs and existing cognitive structures. If input is precisely congruent with existing structure, accommodation of the structure does not occur; and if the input does not fit the structure at all, it simply is not assimilated. Undisguised escape and avoidance behaviors are common in the latter situation, but there are at least two other possibilities: (1) reversion to "learning in the narrow sense"—i.e., learning without understanding—and (2) assimilation to structures very different from those in the mind of the teacher. Both of those occur much more often than educators would like to believe!

The optimal difficulty of a task, then, is one in which the complexity of a cognitive structure almost, but not quite, matches that of an input pattern. Given those conditions, the structure will change in such a way as to produce a closer approximation of perfect equilibrium—a state of the system in which all possible input patterns can be assimilated without distortion.

Perfect equilibrium, however, is an unattainable ideal; it exists only as one end of a theoretical continuum. Moreover, even when cognitive structures are in near equilibrium, the equilibrium is a dynamic one in which the structures (1) assimilate all the input they are capable of organizing and (2) accommodate to input patterns if they are already almost congruent. Therefore, if the discrepancy between the new input and the established structure is within the optimal range, learning will occur without external reinforcement. Motivation is intrinsic to the activity itself.

Because of the manifestly unequal relationship between child and adult, however, it is easy for the latter to abort any conflict by providing an authoritative answer to the question being considered. Authoritative answers are entirely appropriate, of course, if it is "social" (arbitrary) knowledge that is being acquired; but if the objective is logico-mathematical knowledge, the child simply has no alternative to recognizing a conflict and constructing a system that will resolve it. If he believes that the number of marbles on a table increases as the units are moved farther away from each other, he may come to agree with an adult who tells him that the number remains the same. But what has he learned from that episode? He has learned to give the "correct" response in that situation; he has also learned that his own judgment is not to be trusted. (Eventually, he may become quite adept at picking up cues from adults—even from the few who do not explicitly tell him—about how "correct" he is.) He has *not* learned conservation of number; the only way he can "learn" that is to *invent* it.

The role of the teacher in developing logico-mathematical knowledge, then, clearly is not that of a dispenser. *It is absolutely impossible to dispense logico-mathematical knowledge.* The teacher's role is rather that of a guide—a guide not of a planned tour but of a genuine exploration. So far as possible, he is a consultant rather than an authority.

An egalitarian relationship is easier to achieve among peers; indeed, it does not need to be achieved, since it already exists. Such a relationship provides a ready-made opportunity for cognitive conflict: whereas an adult's opinion may be treated as an oracle that is not to be questioned, another child's opinion is just one way of looking at things. Piaget sees social interaction among peers as the best opportunity for childish egocentrism to be overcome through the process of coordinating various points of view.

The teacher can capitalize on that opportunity by encouraging social interaction among peers at every level. It is not easy. As Kamii has observed, "situations in which children argue or clash in an opposition of wills are among the most fruitful for helping them overcome their egocentrism," and it is a high art to wring the maximum educative value from such a situation when the children in it are intent upon hitting each other.[1] But it should be done, and it is not always that difficult, for much social interaction concerns the achievement of common goals. If a child has an idea about how he and his companions might advance toward such a goal, he can communicate it to them only by taking *their* frames of reference into account. He must decenter—recognize his own immediate perspective as one among many.

In all of this, the natural course of development is toward equilibrium. Several theorists have developed similar "equilibrium" models to explain motivation. The focus of Piaget's interest has not been motivation, but his model of cognitive development turns out to be also one of motivation—at least so far as cognitive activity is concerned.

A NOTE CONCERNING NONCOGNITIVE FEATURES

The previous paragraph—indeed, the entire section on motivation—brings us face to face with an issue that until now has been lurking in the background: this is a book about cognitive development, and yet it has some implications that are not as cognitive as they are affective and conative. A review of this section on principles of teaching will reveal references to curiosity, autonomy, purpose, effect, confidence, and motivation. Those terms have not been introduced gratuitously; the concepts to which they refer are inevitable accompaniments of those that I have set out to discuss—indeed, they arise from different views of the same phenomena.

The noncognitive implications of cognitive functioning may be something of a nuisance to an author dealing with a theory of cognitive development, but they should be a real boon to a teacher dealing with a "whole child," because more aspects of his being can be understood from a single frame of reference—or, as by now you probably would prefer, can be "assimilated to the same structure." (In point of fact, Piaget has written on moral development *per se*, and Lawrence Kohlberg has elaborated six stages of moral development within a framework of Piagetian theory).[2] In most situations, conditions that are good for cognitive development also facilitate progress toward moral and more generally, socio-emotional maturity.

CONCLUSION

Although Piaget does not think of himself as an educator, he has been prevailed upon, from time to time, to make some comments about education. The following quotation seems appropriate as a conclusion to this section on principles of teaching:

> The principal goal of education is to create men who are capable of doing new things, not simply of repeating what other generations have done—men who are creative, inventive, and discoverers. The second goal of education is to form minds which can be critical, can verify, and not accept everything they are offered.[3]

He goes on to suggest that if we want active, inventive, critical, autonomous adults, we had better find ways to foster those qualities in our children. That is what this section has been about; the next will examine some recent efforts to make it work.

TEACHING: EXAMPLES

The events depicted in this section are described in considerable detail. You will notice that the descriptions have been liberally laced with interpretations. If, while reading, you will keep in mind the principles delineated in the previous section, you may be able to add some interpretations of your own.

PREPARING THE PREOPERATIONAL CHILD FOR CONCRETE OPERATIONS: KAMII ET AL.

Constance Kamii is an associate professor in the College of Education at the University of Illinois at Chicago Circle and holds a joint appointment with the University of Geneva. For the past 10 years she has done curriculum research on the application of Piaget's theory to teaching in preschool classrooms. During that period, she spent a total of 38 months studying and teaching at the University of Geneva and doing research at the International Center of Genetic Epistemology. She continues to do curriculum research, in collaboration with Rheta DeVries, at a day-care center at the University of Illinois. The Chicago Circle day-care center has been described as "the only preschool . . . which [Piaget] himself has approved."[4] For the sake of simplicity, the following discussion will omit reference to Kamii's collaborators, including DeVries, who is coauthor of the article that will be cited most frequently here ("Piaget for Early Education," *in* R. K. Parker, ed., *The Preschool in Action*, 2nd ed., Allyn & Bacon, 1975) and of a forthcoming book (to be published by Prentice-Hall under the tentative title *Piaget for Early Education*) that is an expanded version of that article.

Kamii begins by placing the preschool within the context of the total development of the child into adulthood. She cites Piaget's remarks (see quotation on p. 147) in setting her long-term objectives but emphasizes the importance of taking each stage as it comes instead of attempting to teach children to think like adults. She specifically condemns the teaching of Piagetian assessment tasks, because she fears that such teaching will result in the learning of correct answers rather than the building of cognitive structures—structures that, in the absence of such teaching, naturally *generate* correct answers.[5]

More immediate objectives fall into three categories: cognitive, socio-emotional, and perceptual-motor. The perceptual-motor objectives are adapted from those of the traditional nursery school and from the work of Frostig and of Kephart; but the socio-emotional objectives are derived indirectly and the cognitive ones directly from Piaget's theory.[6] They are pertinent, therefore, to this discussion.

Socio-emotional Objectives and Strategies

The objectives in the socio-emotional realm are three:

1) Relations with adults
   "To feel secure in egalitarian relationship with adults."

2) Relations with peers
   "To respect the feelings and rights of others and begin

to coordinate different points of view (decentering and cooperating).

3) Autonomy

"To be independent, alert, and curious, to use initiative in pursuing curiosities, to have confidence in his ability to figure out things for himself, and to speak with conviction."[7]

If those look familiar, it's probably because you have been reading the traditional child-development literature, and those objectives *are* similar to some of the traditional ones. Kamii is aware of that similarity, and she defends it by pointing out an important difference: her list comes not from an arbitrary "bag of virtues"[8] but from a body of theory and research. That is an important difference, because "when the teacher understands the theoretical network in which each objective rests in interdependence with the others, the reasons for the objective take on an explicit coherence supported by research evidence."[9]

Attainment of the first objective—an egalitarian relationship with adults—is especially difficult with children as young as those who are Kamii's special concern. She recognizes, as does Piaget, the necessity of coercion in many adult-child interactions. But wherever it is possible to do so, the child should be given an opportunity to make his own decisions; for it is from those decisions, and not from adult coercion or preaching, that he will construct a healthy self-concept and a mature system of morality.

Even when coercion is necessary, it is sometimes possible to promote an egalitarian relationship. Kamii cites an example in which a child tears a book.

The teacher may say, Look, that's *my* book I put out for everybody to enjoy. If it were *your* book, you could do anything you please with it. But since it's *my* book, I will lend it only to the children who can take care of it. . . . Note

> that the teacher here is being coercive but is also putting
> herself on the same level as the child. She is saying to him
> that he has the right to do whatever *he* wants with *his*
> belongings. She is likewise saying that she has the right to do
> whatever she wants with her belongings.[10]

Again, the reason for an egalitarian relationship is to place the child in a position that requires him to make a decision—or if not that, at least to become aware of the issue at hand rather than merely of the power to which he ultimately must accede.

The second objective, "relations with peers," might seem to be mistitled [the title is mine, not Kamii's] were it not for our previous discussion (pp. 144–145) concerning the advantage of peer-group interactions in decentering and in coordinating points of view. Because of the difficulty of establishing egalitarian relations between children and adults, those changes are most likely to occur while children are interacting with each other. Our concern in the *Principles* section was with cognitive development, but here we are once again reminded of the multifaceted nature of the structures that are developing. For although we are now interested in the socio-emotional rather than the cognitive side, the prescription is still the same: find some object or event that is of mutual interest to several children, and encourage them to exchange views about it.

The strategy on the third objective (autonomy) is to encourage the child to be "independent, alert, and curious"—to support him subtly when he shows independence and to honor his convictions. His convictions often will be wrong, but his "wrong" thinking at this stage is a necessary prerequisite to more elaborate constructions later. And once again, "cognitive" and "socio-emotional" are two ways of looking at the same phenomena. Cognitive development is not possible without a measure of autonomy; and communication, cooperation, and morality—not to mention autonomy itself—are manifestations of cognitive development.

Cognitive Objectives and Strategies

There are two objectives for cognitive development:

1) "To come up with interesting ideas, problems, and questions."

2) "To put things into relationship and notice similarities and differences."[11]

On the path defined by the first objective, an opportunity to advance is ready-made: like the young of other primate species, children like to play. Play, according to Piaget, is "an assimilation of reality into the self"[12]—an assimilation that usually leads to some kind of overt activity. In other primate species, play provides opportunities to try activities that under different circumstances might be prohibited—either deliberately by other animals in the troop or simply by the press of attending to more serious matters.[13] Play often functions the same way among humans, when the adults of the species do not prevent it.

To make the most of the developmental opportunities of childhood, some adult intervention is necessary; but it should be subtle and unobtrusive. One way to promote "interesting ideas, problems, and questions" is closely related to play and has already been discussed here in at least two other contexts: let the child be wrong. For if he is not chastised for being wrong, he will be wrong in interesting ways; and in addition to the robust confidence in himself that is one of Kamii's socio-emotional objectives, cognitive progress can be expected. Kamii often has observed that later wrong responses show more congruence with the structure of reality (as adults experience it) than earlier ones do. The inference that she draws from those observations is that Piaget is right when he says that logical thinking evolves without external reinforcement of correct responses. Equilibration, not reinforcement, guides that evolution.

When Kamii states as an objective "to put *things* into relationship . . .," she means precisely that. In the Preoperational

Period, *objects* form the content of thought, and no substitute will suffice. Moreover, it is important to teach to content as well as to process. Kamii refers to some educators' overemphasis on process, or "cognitive skills," as "trying to put more gears into the [information-processing] machine and make mechanical adjustments,"[14] and she admits to a previous error on that point:

> One of our own earlier empiricist mistakes was to assume that since the child had a certain logico-mathematical structure, all he had to do afterward was *apply* this logico-mathematical machine to all kinds of objects. Now, however, we realize that the thinking about objects *is* the structure. Structure does not exist apart from content.[15]

Kamii is, of course, by no means the first to advocate using real objects in the classroom. But the usual reason for such a recommendation is that young children cannot manipulate representations of objects (words, pictures, etc.). Kamii's position is that even if they are able to manipulate representations, children still should interact with real objects; her reason is that "since knowledge is constructed by acting on reality and transforming it, children *have to* deal with reality itself, and words and pictures cannot substitute."[16]

The final point about contents is that they are not merely objects and information; they are "ideas about what to do with objects and information."[17] Kamii quotes Piaget to the effect that while a child may on occasion become interested in some activity like classifying or seriating for its own sake, he is more likely to perform those operations in the service of some other goal; the implication is that their occurrence under the latter circumstance is as beneficial as under the former and that it requires less intrusion into the child's plans of action. She cites "marbles" as an example, pointing out that marbles can be "merely observed, described, and sorted as objects,"[18] but that they also can be used to play various games that require those activities [e.g., separating large from small, heavy from light, "steelies" from "glassies," etc.] plus others [e.g., constructing relationships between each of those attributes and the behavior of the marbles as they are hitting or being hit]. "There is thus no clear distinction in a Piagetian curriculum between 'content' and 'process' in the usual sense. It is only when there is something intrinsically interesting that children are alert and curious. They make connections when there is something real and interesting to think about. The connections they make *are* indeed their logico-mathematical framework."[19]

Mention has been made of "classification" and "seriation," which are, of course, concrete operations. Preschool children may occasionally attain that level of functioning, but they do so very seldom, and Kamii explicitly disavows any intention of "teaching concrete operations." When she states as an objective that the child will "notice similarities and differences," she is describing prerequisites to concrete operations, not the operations themselves. Once more the child is encouraged to think in his own way about things. If he does that, he will be building the structures that will make it possible for him to think later in a different way—a more advanced way that again is his own.

Although her stated objectives do not reveal it, Kamii does admit the need for "social" (arbitrary) knowledge: the child needs to know the folkways of his culture. But the Piagetian emphasis is clearly elsewhere, and Kamii is distressed when the traditional school turns its attention to those other matters and treats them as if they, too, were "social" knowledge.

The objective "to put things into relationships . . ." cannot be reached by such methods. It is important, according to Kamii, to make distinctions among the kinds of knowledge, because each demands a different kind of teaching. The acquisition of logico-mathematical knowledge, for example, requires the invention of relationships by the child, and the attempt to teach it to him "through social feedback usually results in the 'pasting on' of correct answers to the child's genuine way of thinking."[20] (Incidentally, as was mentioned in the Principles section, and as Kamii pointed out in relation to her socio-emotional objectives, the learning of such "pasted on" answers certainly will contribute nothing to the child's confidence in his ability to figure things out for himself; it may even shake whatever confidence he already has.) We have returned once again to the necessity of a child's being wrong before he can be right. The social transmission of right answers won't circumvent that law, as the following example demonstrates:

> For example, when the four-year old tells us that there are more brown beads than beads, he is expressing his own conviction. To the child who compares six brown beads with two white ones, there are indeed more brown ones than white ones. If the adult imposes his authority to correct the logical relationships the child has created for himself, the child may end up learning that six brown beads are *not* more than two white ones. If he has not yet constructed the structure for comparing the class of beads with its subclasses, he cannot understand the correction. . . .[21]

In the light of Piaget's conception of the relation of language to thinking, Kamii takes particular umbrage at the attempts being made by some educators to effect the social transmission of logico-mathematical knowledge by giving children verbal tools for thinking. "Telling words that designate relationships (such as 'more-less,' 'between,' and 'smooth-rough') seems particularly to make teachers feel that they must be giving the children the tools they need for abstract thinking";[22] whereas actually, the words are only as good as the structures to which they are assimilated, so they can serve as "tools" only *after* the structure has been fashioned by coordinating actions in the real world. Returning to the beads problem, Kamii observes that

> when we perceive reality (beads in this example), we perceive it by assimilating it into a logico-mathematical framework. Therefore, sensory information about 'brown beads' and 'beads' can be only as good as our logico-mathematical framework. Preoperational children have no trouble perceiving 'brown beads' and 'beads,' and they do not have any trouble understanding the words involved. Their problem, therefore, lies in their logico-mathematical framework, which can be built only by reflecting abstraction [logico-mathematical experience].[23]

She goes on to say that after Piagetian testing of hundreds of subjects from four to sixteen years of age she is (1) convinced that their cognitive problems are not due to deficiencies of language and (2) appalled at "the unnecessarily big words older children dish out in profusion, showing a thick coat of 'school varnish' that serves as a straightjacket around their minds."[24]

Apparently *words* are not the answer.

Children in Kamii's classroom are perpetually active—overtly so in most cases—because she believes with Piaget that the development of intelligence is the organization of actions. Provision is made for all kinds of experience (physical, logico-mathematical, and social), and except for the folkways of the culture and the necessities of physical safety, the child is permitted to do things *his* way. When he does so, discrepancies occur—discrepancies among his cognitive structures and between them and reality. Eventually, his awareness of those discrepancies motivates him to reorganize his structures in such a way as to restore relative equilibrium. By being "wrong" in a manner appropriate to his stage of development, the child prepares himself for the integration of current structures into later ones that are more elaborate and sophisticated.

PREPARING THE CONCRETE OPERATIONAL CHILD FOR FORMAL OPERATIONS: RENNER ET AL.

John W. Renner has been professor of science education at the University of Oklahoma since 1962. He has taught science at every level, from kindergarten through the master's degree in physics. He has served as the Associate Executive Secretary of the National Science Teachers Association and has directed a field trial and research center for the Science Curriculum Improvement Study. It was the SCIS experience that convinced Renner of the importance of Piaget's model to both curriculum development and teaching methodology. Renner's research over the past decade has focused upon the measurement of students' intellectual levels and upon the design of curricula to promote their intellectual development, and he has written four college textbooks that emphasize the utility of Piagetian theory in teaching. For the sake of simplicity, the following discussion will omit reference to Renner's collaborators, including Don G. Stafford, who is coauthor of the book that will be cited most frequently here (*Teaching Science in the Secondary Schools*, Harper & Row, 1972).

Renner and his associates probably would be pleased to see "inquiry" methods used throughout the school. Indeed, in at least one study they have demonstrated the beneficial effects of inquiry activities on reading, mathematics, and social studies, as measured by standard achievement tests of paragraph meaning, mathematics, and the application of such skills as the use of maps and globes in the solution of problems in social studies.[25] Even in that study, however, the effects were not the direct results of inquiry programs in reading, mathematics, and social studies; they were the side effects of a four-year program in *science*.

A science program was chosen by the Oklahoma group partly because their own backgrounds were in various scientific disciplines; but there is another reason, too. Science is itself a method of inquiry (as well as a body of knowledge), and it provides a thoroughly tested model thereof. The following section provides a quick look at that model, followed by a description of its application to a specific educational problem.

The Nature of Inquiry

Renner offers alternative conceptualizations of scientific inquiry, all of which are necessarily closely related.[26] The one to be examined here is organized around the notions of *exploration, invention*, and *discovery* and is illustrated by the work of Wilhelm Konrad Röntgen.[27]

On November 8, 1895, Röntgen was preparing to duplicate some experiments on the effects of cathode rays (the rays emitted from the negative electrode of a partially evacuated Crookes tube). He wished to observe the luminescence caused in certain substances when held in the path of the rays; from earlier work, he knew that the rays would travel only about 5 centimeters in air. To facilitate handling, he prepared the materials as thin coatings on sheets of paper; to observe the luminescence to best advantage, he used cardboard to cover the part of the Crookes tube from which light could escape. With the tube in operation, he turned off the laboratory lights to determine how lightproof his covering was and was astonished to see a faint but unmistakable glow at the far end of his laboratory bench! The glow came from one of the sheets he had coated with a luminescent material.

Here was a discrepancy between what his cognitive structure had led him to expect and what he actually observed. His previous explorations, and those of others, had convinced him (1) that Crookes tubes emit cathode rays and only cathode rays and (2) that cathode rays travel no farther than about 5 centimeters in air. He explored further, checking his observations in various ways. When the apparatus was switched off, the glow disappeared; when he switched it on again, the glow reappeared. He even took the sheet of coated paper into the next room, closed the door, and darkened that room. The sheet still glowed when the tube was operating.

More observations followed (the discrepancy was so motivating that he locked himself in his laboratory for several days), but observations alone were not to resolve the discrepancy. For that, an *invention* was needed. If cathode rays travel only 5 centimeters in air, and if a luminescent substance glows when placed beyond the range of the cathode rays from a Crookes tube, then there must be *another* ray coming from the tube. Röntgen invented the x-ray.

Exploration, invention, and discovery do not form a series of neatly separated activities, for exploration both precedes and follows invention, and insofar as invention is extended in time, the two may occur simultaneously. On the other hand, once an invention has been made, it serves as a focus of explorations that may produce discoveries. Röntgen and others have made many discoveries about x-rays. He found, for example, that they easily penetrate such widely different materials as wood and flesh, that they partially penetrate bone, and that they are completely stopped by lead. Medical personnel soon discovered the positive contribution that x-rays could make to their profession, and they have much more recently discovered the hazards of too much exposure.

Inquiry as an Educative Process

In the example just given, we tend to think of Röntgen as a scientist making a contribution to his discipline, but it is just as accurate to think of him as a student of science whose inquiry led to a refinement of his cognitive structures. Advocates of an inquiry approach to education hold that the restructuring process is essentially the same in *any* student—that intellectual development involves the same processes of exploration, invention, and discovery no matter whether its product is or is not a significant addition to a collective body of knowledge. Inquiry, then, is the same for the student as it is for the scientist. There are some deviations from that rule, as will be shown presently, but in general the student is invited to *learn* science by *doing* science in essentially the same way a scientist would.

A task assigned to a high school biology class is offered as an example.[28] The topic is taxonomy:

If there is to be a classification of organisms, there must be a collection of organisms to classify. The students make their own collections in the organisms' natural habitat; they are *exploring* both the organisms and the habitat. In this example, the organisms are insects; hundreds of insects are captured and brought into the laboratory.

There, the entire set (insects) is sorted into subsets. The students' task is very similar to a Piagetian test of classification, in which the subject is asked to "place together all those that are alike in some way." Since the first sorting results in subsets that although alike in one way are different in other ways, additional sortings are necessary. The result is a hierarchical system for identifying insects. That system is an *invention*.

Not only is that particular taxonomic system invented, but so is the notion of taxonomy itself. Once the students have acquired that notion, they set about *discovering* what it can do: plants and other animals in the immediate geographical area are assimilated to it, and its structure is accommodated to fit the new conditions. The discussion that accompanies all this turns eventually to the adaptive functions of the features that are being examined and hence to the notion of evolutionary "purpose."

The teaching objectives here are both cognitive and non-cognitive. In cognitive terms, the primary objective is the development of an understanding of taxonomy as a classification of organisms according to their evolutionary interrelationships; other cognitive benefits accrue in the form of information and of problem-solving strategies that students acquire as a result of "the process of handling, observing, measuring, and, in general, getting to know the organisms they are using to form this taxonomy . . .,"[29] and noncognitive gains in autonomy and confidence emerge from those same activities.

The most important functions of the teacher in all of this are to get the investigation started and to keep it going.[30] He may ascertain initially what subject matter the students would *like* to study, or he may decide in advance what they *should* study. Either way, the hoped-for knowledge is seen as a construction by each student rather than a gift from the teacher.

The teacher, according to Renner, is responsible for providing students with access to appropriate materials, occasional "cues and clues," and time.[31] In the biology example, the organisms in their habitat constitute the major material resource, and of course the classifying activity takes time. (The *amount* of time devoted to a topic is determined by "what is going on and the educational value of it"[32] rather than by a syllabus or textbook.) The matter of "cues and clues" requires some elaboration.

You may recall, from the discussion of Kamii's work, that unless a young child's autonomy is respected when he is confronting a problem, he will learn to interpret as confirmation or disconfirmation even very subtle cues that he gets from an adult. The result is often more guessing than thinking.

Cues of that kind are *not* what Renner has in mind when he says that a secondary school teacher should provide "cues and clues." ("Clue" is probably the better term.) Instead of being used to reinforce a correct response, thus encouraging guesses, clues are used to suggest other possibilities, thus encouraging thought. It is true that giving away answers robs the student of the opportunity to find or invent or discover them for himself; it is also true, however, that students sometimes "become hopelessly stuck,"[33] and their motivation wanes unless some progress seems imminent. It is the teacher's responsibility to get them moving again.

That does not mean that students are prevented from making mistakes; they, like younger children, should be encouraged to follow the plan of investigation that seems most logical to *them*. Often such a plan proves fruitful; but if it does not,

> . . . that fact will most likely be discovered, either because the data produced do not make sense or because the investigation itself cannot be pushed to completion with the operational plan with which it was begun. In either case, such a situation clearly demonstrates the need for informed, adult assistance. The teacher needs to step into the investigation at this point and review with the students how they reached the point at which they are. Often in such a review the learners themselves will see that they had begun their search upon an incorrect assumption or wrong information. If not, the teacher needs to suggest to them an alternate way of thinking about the original problem that will ultimately lead them to a redesign of the investigation, which they then will be able to pursue to completion, and which will then provide them with usable data. This does not mean providing learners with an answer. This is simply a method of refocusing attention upon the problem being considered.[34]

In the biology example, once the specimens have been assembled in the laboratory, the students might have difficulty getting started with their classification. If so, the class may be separated into smaller groups, and the teacher may suggest to one group that its members consider the number of legs on the animal, to another that they count the wings, and to a third that they inspect the mouth parts. The precise nature of the suggestion is not important, really; because while they are pursuing one possibility, others will occur to the investigators *without* further suggestions. The function of the clue is to keep things moving; if the students are confident (and if they do not expect answers from the teacher), they will solve the problem by themselves.

The emphasis on "keeping things going" is an emphasis on action—or, more accurately, on construction through action, for the students are constantly building systems for processing information. In the biology example, the action began with the collection of specimens in their natural habitat (physical experience) and continued through the construction of a taxonomic system (logico-mathematical experience). The sequential integration of structures was accomplished by taking into account each student's level of development. The research of Renner and his colleagues[35] and the studies of several other workers[36] have indicated that most adolescents entering high school probably are concrete operational thinkers. In the biology example, therefore, it was appropriate that the core activity was classification—a concrete operation. When the students were sorting insects according to various physical characteristics, they were engaged in concrete operations. When they were formulating the reasons for making their classifications, however—particularly when those reasons had to do with the relation of physical features to the survival of the animals and ultimately to the theory of evolution—they were engaged in formal thinking. And when they imposed their abstract model (the taxonomy) onto the real world, they were thinking formally again. If this analysis is correct, the teacher should find ways of avoiding prolonged participation of concrete operational thinkers in tasks that require formal operations for their successful completion. A less serious hazard is the prolonged participation of formal operational students in concrete operational tasks. In the biology example, a correct match might be accomplished by encouraging concrete operational thinkers to do more detailed classifications (concrete operations are the foundations of formal thought) while those who are already operating at the formal level turn their attention to the rationale of the taxonomy and its application to insects not yet encountered. With adequate attention to the developmental levels of students and the matching of tasks to provide optimal discrepancy and cognitive conflict, motivation should take take care of itself. In Renner's experience, that is indeed what happens.

TESTING

Piaget's theory is based upon extensive observations of the behavior of children and adolescents. His method of observation is quite different from that of traditional mental testing, but both are systematic, and both are concerned with mental development. It should therefore not be at all surprising to find that a new test is currently being standardized—a test that has its roots in Piaget's theory and incorporates his method.

The new test ("scale of mental development") is the product of a program of research initiated several years ago by Monique Laurendeau and Adrien Pinard in the laboratory of genetic psychology at the University of Montreal.[37] The product is an attempt to combine the advantages of Piaget's method (thoroughness and flexibility of questioning) with those of traditional psychometric methods (standardization of questioning).

A NEW KIND OF INTELLIGENCE TEST

Although most intelligence tests today do not make any direct use of the concept of "mental age,"* they are all descendants of the original Binet scale in which mental age was the very heart of the whole process. But the concept of mental age bears little relationship to the Piagetian "stage" of development, so a Piagetian test would necessarily be different in a very important way.

If we were to compare the new test with the Stanford-Binet, for example, we would find that in the latter, items have met a statistical criterion of discrimination between chronological age

---

*"Mental age" is a scale unit that was until recently the basis of scoring Stanford-Binet intelligence tests. The average child of four has a mental age of four; the average child of six has a mental age of six, etc. A child's IQ is the ratio of his mental age to his chronological age at the time of the test (MA/CA); e.g., if his test performance is equal to that of the average six-year-old but he is only five, his IQ will be 120. That is, 6/5 1.20 (the decimal is dropped). Although the "ratio IQ" is no longer used, the concept of mental age is still fundamental to all Binet-type testing.

groups; that is, older subjects have tended to pass them, younger ones to fail them. The difficulty level of any item is the chronological age of the youngest group of subjects who can pass it.

In contrast, the first step in the Montreal test has been a thorough study of intellectual development—a study based upon and including Piaget's own observations. Test items have been derived from that study and from the theory that spawned it. They have been designed specifically to reveal the dominant aspects of each stage of development. Only after all that has been accomplished is a statistical analysis performed to ascertain the chronological age at which each ability is acquired.

The administration of a traditional intelligence test is highly structured. With few exceptions, the same questions are asked of every subject on each item of the test. (*A sample item:* Tell me what's wrong with the following sentence: "The judge said to the prisoner, 'You are to be hanged, and I hope it will be a warning to you!'") An exception would occur if an additional question were introduced when the response to the standard question has been ambiguous; for the purpose of every question is to classify the subject's response as "pass" or "fail." Once that objective has been achieved, the examiner moves on to the next item. Given the rationale of the previous paragraph, all that is as it should be.

But another rationale is possible. If performance is conceived as a manifestation of a stage in the evolution of intelligence instead of a statistical average, it becomes important to find out *why* a particular subject is responding in a particular way, even if that response is wrong; in fact, a wrong answer can be more revealing in the long term than a correct one. Each question presents an opportunity for the subject to respond in a manner that will reveal the quality of his thinking, and the content of each is determined by the subject's response to the preceding ones. (An "item" in the Montreal test is likely to consist of doing an "experiment" in view of the subject—e.g., the floating bodies problem—and then questioning him about what he has just seen.) The entire testing session is therefore much less rigidly structured than is customary in psychometrics.

"Psychometrics" means "psychological measurement," and

measurement implies quantification. Quantification was alluded to above when we discussed the difficulty level of a conventional test item. It would be possible to make difficulty level
count directly in the total score, but in the Stanford-Binet that
is not done; instead, each item that is passed is given the same
score, regardless of its difficulty. It is true that the items are
arranged in order of increasing difficulty and that for any given
subject records are kept only of those between the all-passed
level and the all-failed level. But it is also true that within those
limits it is possible to compensate for failing certain low-level
items by passing certain high-level items.

The possibility of such compensation emphasizes the fact that
a "mental age" from the Stanford-Binet is not a true genetic
stage that depends for its existence upon a mastery of the
acquisitions characteristic of all preceding stages. The final
score is instead merely a sum of items passed in a series of generally increasing difficulty.

The scoring of the Montreal scale can be characterized
quickly by contrasting it with that of the Stanford-Binet.
Whereas the latter allows for compensatory achievements at
higher levels than those at which failures already have occurred,
the Montreal method usually requires classifying the subject into
a developmental stage by means of a qualitative analysis of his
performance. Whereas the final result of a Stanford-Binet test
is a score determined by the number of items passed within a
limited range of difficulty,* the issue of a Montreal test is a
statement about the subject's level of intellectual development—
a statement that expresses the quality of his responses to a
relatively small number of problem situations. Whereas the
Stanford-Binet presents the same questions (within the appropriate range of difficulty) to all subjects, the Montreal test presents different, alternative questions to each subject. The choice
in each case depends on the subject's responses to earlier questions.

The relationships discussed above are summarized in Table III.

---

*An experienced examiner may glean a great deal more information from
the testing session, but it is not a part of the basic validation of the instrument.

TABLE III. RELATION OF MONTREAL INTELLIGENCE TEST TO TRADI-
TIONAL TYPE

Characteristic of Test	Type of Test	
	Traditional	Montreal
Standardization	"Level" determined statistically.	"Level" derived from theory.
	Items selected that discriminate between specified chronological age groups.	Intellectual development studied; problems devised to reveal various levels of mental process. Statistical analysis, to determine average age of each acquisition, is done later.
Administration	Highly structured. With few exceptions, same questions asked of all subjects who respond to a given item.	Less structured. Each question determined by subject's answer to preceding ones.
	Exceptions are questions designed to clarify pass-fail distinction.	Questions designed to reveal quality of subject's thinking.
	Only right answers are important.	Wrong answers are important too.
Scoring	Determined by number of items passed within a limited range of difficulty.	Determined by quality of responses to a standard set of items. "Level" is quality of response rather than difficulty of items passed.
	Failing an item at one level can be compensated for by passing one at a different level.	Items not passed or failed, but evaluated for stage inclusion.

TESTING IN THE SCHOOL

The prime objective of the Montreal research was to extend Piaget's observations to populations other than that of Geneva under conditions imposed by the canons of experimental method. Laurendeau and Pinard wanted to know whether Piaget's stages would survive that kind of scrutiny. (In general, they did.) The development of an intelligence scale for use in the schools was only a by-product of a program of research in "pure" or "basic" science.

The fact remains that one result of that research has been an ordinal scale* of mental development applicable to children from two to twelve years of age. Like the "spin-off" of the NASA space program, the result could be as important a technological advance as if it had been sought directly.

We have already alluded to the potential effect of Piaget's theory on teaching. Nothing more need be said here, beyond simply pointing out that for the teacher who wishes to implement Piagetian ideas, it is essential to ascertain the developmental level of the students being taught. There are other ways in which that might be accomplished; teachers familiar with the theory can to some extent make their own judgments. But a standardized test could prove extremely helpful, provided that the teacher is able to converse in Piagetian terms with the specialist who administers the test.

It is clear that such a test would require the services of a specialist. Furthermore, a specialist would have to be more than a mere technician, for the unstructured format demands a thorough grounding in the theory that underlies each question. Who might the specialist be?

The person who is at once available and psychologically trained is the school psychologist. For the most part, training in school psychology has not included much acquaintance with Piaget's theory or procedures; but the development of a standardized Piagetian scale of intelligence could change all that. In

---

*An ordinal scale is one that places items in order without using equal units or an absolute zero.

fact, it might even significantly affect the character of school psychology as a professional discipline. There has been a recent trend away from testing as the prime function of the profession, and toward more involvement in the process of education in the classroom. The new test could precipitate a fusion of those two functions. The school psychologist is the person in the school who knows the most about how children think, and who therefore would be drawn into the classroom as a more active, specialized participant in the educational process.

Finally, a Piaget-inspired scale of intelligence could facilitate research on questions of practical concern. "The psychology of the exceptional child," for example, could be expected to have immediate impact on "the education of the exceptional child." It may turn out that reading and writing disabilities can be traced to the distortion of certain fundamental representations, or even of prerepresentational structures, and that the same is true of the more generalized disabilities known as "mental retardation." Programs might be devised for "gifted" children that would take advantage of their gifts without interfering with the harmony and integration of "normal" development. Counselors would profit from a clarification of the nature of aptitudes. And everyone in the school would benefit from a deeper understanding of children's thinking in general.

FURTHER COMMENTS AND RESIDUAL QUESTIONS

In the foregoing sections, I have been concerned with the more-or-less direct effect of Piaget's theory on educational practice, and have examined some examples thereof. But regardless of the specific techniques that have emerged or eventually might emerge from all of this theory-inspired activity, a genuinely professional person can realize an immediate gain by studying the theory itself. A theory may serve as a framework onto which both old and new facts will fit and as a blueprint that will explicate the interrelationships among those facts. In Piagetian terms, one might think of it as a kind of super-scheme ready to assimilate whatever is relevant to it. Such a scheme makes it possible for the teacher to analyze the child in terms of the operations of which he is capable at that particular time and to analyze the task in terms of the operations required to perform it. He might then combine the two in such a way as to produce optimal discrepancy, which would ensure high motivation, much activity, and a maximum of change in cognitive structure. The dedicated teacher may also hope for a gain quite apart from the success of his own interventions in the developmental process: he may hope to attain the kind of satisfaction that comes to the anthropologist who has studied a preliterate culture until he actually understands how its people think.

The ideas that I have presented concerning applications, however, are extremely tentative; and one should not overlook their limitations. In the remainder of this chapter I shall discuss some of those limitations and point to some issues that remain unresolved.

It is not difficult to find a possible limitation to the application most recently discussed: the amount of time required of a highly competent professional person to test a single child by the Montreal method is truly formidable. Pinard and Laurendeau report that in their standardization project, the average individual testing time was 10 hours.[38] The routine use of test reports in the planning of classroom activities would represent a formidable obstacle to Piagetian testing in the schools. The primary objective of the Montreal project, however, was to learn more about children's thinking rather than to develop a practical instrument for educators. For the latter purpose, the Montreal battery is excessively thorough; it is essential that some sort of compromise be reached between the flexibility and richness of the clinical method on the one hand and the demands of time and objectivity on the other. The Montreal approach is only a partial answer, but some attention is being given to the problem, even in Geneva, where a standardization project is in progress under the direction of Bärbel Inhelder and Vinh Bang.[39] In the English-speaking countries, several attempts have been made to develop a practical scale.[40] They have met with varying degrees of success. One of the most convincing demonstrations of practical utility is a study by Kaufman and Kaufman[41] in which scores on their battery (13 tasks organized into 5 tests of concrete operations) were used to predict achievement (as measured by the Stanford Achievement Tests) in the first grade. Their battery required less than 25 minutes of testing time per child; the correlation with the criterion was .64 by itself (as compared to .58 for Lorge-Thorndike mental age by itself) and .69 when *combined* with the Lorge-Thorndike. Those results suggest that the Piagetian tests (1) compare favorably with the Lorge-Thorndike—a traditional "IQ test"—in predicting school achievement as defined in this study and (2) measure somewhat different abilities than the traditional test. Because the Piagetian tests measure different mental abilities than conventional intelligence tests, their best use may be as supplements to, rather than replacements for, conventional materials. That is what Kaufman and Kaufman's multiple correlation of .69* suggests; the new British Intelligence Scale[42] uses them in that way; and individual clinicians of course may do their own supplementing. A dilemma remains for the psychometrician, however: there are many sophisticated operations that he cannot perform on test results unless those results are reported as *scores*; but the more closely the outcome of a Piagetian assessment resembles a simple score, the less closely it resembles the *description* of mental processes that Piaget intended it to be.

At least one British[44] and several American[45] studies have indicated that Piaget's norms for the achievement of formal operations (see page 20) probably are not valid for British and

---

*Kaufman and Kaufman's finding that the Piaget and Lorge-Thorndike tests together predict achievement better than either by itself is by no means the only evidence that the former, while having much in common with "IQ tests," measures something that the conventional tests do not. Other investigations, including both regression and factor-analytic studies, have come to the same conclusion.[43]

American populations.* In every one of those studies, the age suggested by Piaget has proven to be too low, and many individuals have failed to reach the formal level at *any* age. Karplus and Karplus,[46] for example, report that formal thinking was used by only 15 percent of college preparatory students in grades 10 through 12 and that the percentage was no higher in a sample of adults; and McKinnon and Renner, using different tests, found that "almost 75 percent" of their sample of entering college freshmen "were either partially or completely concrete operational in their thinking"—that only about one-fourth of them thought consistently in a way that could be classified with any degree of confidence as "formal."[47]

Whatever the median age turns out to be for any designated group, there are sure to be wide individual differences within each age category. Those differences are to be expected; different individuals should pass through the stages at different rates, and it should not be surprising to find some who do not reach the more advanced stages at all. Nevertheless, when an individual subject demonstrates concrete operational thinking in one content area and formal thinking in another, there is cause for concern; for, as Flavell puts it, Piaget's "lifelong professional goal has been to find . . . structural wholes, of great abstraction and generality, which currently identify the essence of organized intelligence at its various levels."[50] Ideally, such structural wholes ("metastructures," I have called them) should be capable of assimilating *any* appropriate content. Piaget has recognized the resistance of some contents to assimilation: he has coined the term *horizontal décalage* to refer to the phenomenon. ("Décalage" means "uncoupling" or "displacement." The term "horizontal" is intended to suggest that the successive applications of a structure to different contents all occur "at the same level" of development.† "*Vertical* décalage" refers to the application of struc-

---

*The subjects on which Piaget's norms are based were "taken from the better schools of Geneva."[48] The British and American deviations from those norms are small compared to those of nonindustrialized societies or even to those of the lower socio-economic classes in Western countries.[49]

†For an example of horizontal décalage, see the plasticene-balls problem

tures to analogous contents at successively higher levels of development—a conception that *is* consistent with the major tenets of the theory.) But the concept has an *ad hoc* quality that calls for further explanation. Piaget has recently discussed the problem and has suggested that "all normal subjects" become capable of formal operations sometime between the ages of 11 and 20, but that they do so "in different areas according to their aptitudes and their professional specializations (advanced studies or different types of apprenticeship for the various trades) . . .";[51] but he has not shown precisely how the concept of horizontal décalage is derived from his general theory.

That is a theoretical issue. When Piaget turns from pure theory to the practical affairs of the classroom, he sometimes seems to subscribe to what I have called a "recapitulation" model of school learning. The teacher "might begin by having the child operate directly on physical entities, then have him proceed to cognitive anticipations and retrospections of operations not actually performed at the moment, and so on, until the originally external actions can take place internally and in complete autonomy from the environment."[52] Although that is a valid account of the series of acquisitions over a period of time extending from the sensorimotor period to the Concrete Operations Period, it may not represent a necessary sequence for every new acquisition of content *within* the Concrete Operations Period or beyond it. In the extreme case, the recapitulation model would require that a college physics student begin his study of mechanics, for example, at the sensorimotor level, continue through the preoperational and concrete operational levels, and only then be ready to deal with the material on a formal level. That would be an extremely inefficient way to teach physics—that is, unless the preliminary steps are very much abbreviated. It is possible that the mature student assimilates sensorimotor information in an instant, without the necessity of actually manipulating the materials, and of course one of the salient features of formal thought is that it consists

(pp. 71–72). Conservation of substance is achieved early in the Concrete Operations Period, whereas weight is not conserved until later in the same period.

of formal *operations on* concrete *operations*. In any case, the *im-mature* learner should be well served by the implementation of Piaget's suggestion just as it stands.

Once a purported learning experience has occurred, how does one ascertain whether it has been successful? Recently it has become fashionable (because of the propagation of simplistic theories of learning, as well as for demographic and political reasons) for members of state legislatures to speak with great conviction about "accountability" in education. Educators have described several kinds of accountability,[53] but politicians usually have only one in mind when they use the term. In their view, education should consist of a setting of detailed behavioral objectives followed by a demonstration that those objectives have been reached. Certainly that view has a strong common-sense appeal, but educators who have been influenced by Piaget's theory believe that it is incomplete—that important outcomes are likely to be ignored in both the setting and the measuring phases, and in fact that those same important out-comes are unlikely even to *occur* as a result of such a procedure. It is true that, as we have said earlier, cognitive organization is an inference from behavior. Difficulty arises, however, when attempts are made to specify, in advance and in great detail, precisely what that behavior will be. Certainly such attempts should not be written off *a priori* as inadequate, but unfortunately the very making of such an attempt tends to bias the educator against those outcomes that are difficult to describe. And how does one describe "the having of wonderful ideas"?[54] More important, how does one encourage the proliferation of ideas if one's primary concern is to demonstrate each child's con-formity to a pre-established set of objectives? The dedicated Piagetian teacher may not be as "accountable" as some would like.

On the other hand, we must recognize that there are in a child's life many occasions for a kind of learning that does not contribute in any direct way to the development of operational intelligence. Children learn very early, for example, "to respect the rights of others." Most kindergarten children never do re-spect the rights of other people, really, for they are incapable of adopting the other's point of view. But they can be conditioned to discriminate certain stimuli from others, to differentiate some responses from others, and to organize those discriminations and differentiations into patterns that superficially resemble respect for the rights of others. For purposes of efficient administration of groups of children, at home or at school, that may be sufficient; it is at the very least helpful! And so it goes with many other acquisitions. Piaget may not be especially concerned with them, but that does not mean that the conscientious parent or teacher need not be.

Even in areas of strictly academic learning, Piaget-inspired procedures have been criticized as inefficient. Such arguments are particularly pertinent when they refer to education at the higher levels. (See my own comments above on "recapitulation.") Ausubel has called for a distinction between "reception" and "discovery" learning—i.e., between (1) "the long-term acquisition and retention of stable, organized, and extensive bodies of meaningful, generalizable knowledge" and (2) "growth in the ability to use this knowledge in the solution of particular problems, including those problems which, when solved, augment the learner's original store of knowledge."[55] He points out that although the two may overlap, they are distinguishable, and he asserts further that "the inductive derivation of concepts and generalizations from diverse instances is . . . only a conspicuous feature of *concept attainment* during *childhood*. . . ."[56] He goes on to say that the acquisition of knowledge is a legitimate objective in its own right and that the goal of the second kind of learning is usually "to facilitate everyday living and decision-making, not to discover knowledge that is of sufficient general significance to merit permanent incorporation in cognitive structure."[57] If Ausubel is right, the Kamii approach is appropriate in the preschool and primary grades but increasingly inappropriate thereafter, for it would certainly take an inordinate amount of time to "discover" the enormous amount of "stable, organized, . . . , meaningful, generalizable knowledge" that must be acquired by anyone who aspires to a general education. In this regard it is interesting to note that in Renner's "inquiry" method, the teacher arranges discrepancies that, it is hoped, will lead to cognitive conflict and the equilibration of new structures; but he (the teacher) does not shrink from intervening at critical points with ready-made "inventions." That procedure is difficult to derive from Piaget's theory, and seems instead to represent an incorporation of the Ausubelian perspective into a teaching method that is essentially Piagetian. It is an incorporation of *guidance* of various kinds and amounts (though the amount is always small in relation to that found in traditional approaches).

That incorporation would do little violence to the theory, it seems to me, if the *kind* of guidance were to vary with the developmental level of the learner. It could change from sensorimotor (e.g., inducing an infant to perform a particular skilled act) to concrete operational (asking him to predict the results of limited transformations that he performs himself) to formal operational (requesting a statement of all possibilities relating to the event). If Ausubel's criticism is to be taken seriously, the *amount* of guidance might vary with level of development and of task difficulty (so that prompts and clues, and even full-blown syntheses, might be included at the higher levels). At any level, Piaget warns, the teacher must beware of "verbalism"—linguistic performance by the student that gives a false impression of operational facility. The conceptual referents of a given linguistic expression may be strikingly different in a child from what they are in his teacher.

That last observation is typical of the Piagetian attitude toward language. Educators sometimes classify the effects of education into two broad categories: (1) physical and quantitative thinking and (2) language and associative processes. Piaget's influence has been confined largely to the first. The reason can be found, I believe, in the theory, which sometimes regards language as merely an epiphenomenon. If the theory is modified (as any viable theory must be), the way in which the theory regards language may be one aspect to undergo modification, for it seems to me that language can serve both as a device for the deployment of attention and as a mechanism for efficient coding of information. Moreover, although language may often function in the *service* of operational intelligence, I suspect that it is sometimes an integral *part* of that intelligence. Piaget has recognized the importance of language, especially in formal operations; but the recognition has been more of a reluctant admission than a triumphant affirmation, and that seeming reluctance probably has influenced those of his disciples who have tried to apply his theory to education. Add that to the dependence on logico-mathematical models to represent intellectual operations and you have a formidable barrier to the application of the theory outside of science and mathematics—at least at the upper levels.

The last criticism that I shall cite here came out of my own ruminations about Piaget's theory in education, but it has occurred independently to several others. It is a proposition that cuts to the heart of that relation: "With respect to the developmental changes with which Piaget's theory is concerned,

1) if a child is not ready to change, no teacher can help him;
2) if he *is* ready, the change will occur *without* intervention;
3) therefore, intervention is superfluous."

Piaget's own view often appears to be in general agreement with that proposition. In fact, at least one quotation seems at first glance even to *extend* it by implying that intervention is not only superfluous but actually harmful: "Every time you teach a child something, you keep him from reinventing it."[58] We do not know, however, how Piaget would define the word "teach," and we do not know whether he would agree with Ausubel that children and adolescents differ in the amount of "reception" learning that is desirable. It is possible to "teach" without "telling," and it may be that students at different developmental levels differ in the amount of "telling" that they can use.

Even if we grant that intervention can be effective (if it is sufficiently subtle), what is the nature of the effect? Specifically, Piaget has addressed himself to the problem of accelerating mental development; and again we find that his attitude is essentially negative. He calls acceleration "the American question," clearly implying that for him it is not a problem at all. To the question "Can we accelerate the stages of development?" Piaget's answer is that we probably can, but that he is not sure that we should. He proffers a "hypothesis" that, he admits, he is so far incapable of proving: that there is an optimal time for the organization of operations.* Then he goes on to compare the development of object permanence in a human baby with that same development in a kitten. The child and the kitten go through the same stages, but what requires nine to twelve months in the child is accomplished in three by the kitten. But is that an advantage to the kitten? Piaget says no, that the additional time was not wasted, because the child will continue to develop after the kitten has stopped. There is an optimal time, but the *opt*imal is not *min*imal.

None of this is very clearly derived from the theory, and just what the optimal time is for any given child in any given stage, says Piaget, remains an unanswered question on which we need a great deal of research.[60] Meanwhile, teachers should do the best they can to provide an environment that will maximize the chances for each child to have whatever experiences he can at his current level of development. Teachers can proceed with the confidence that when a child *can* have a higher-level experience, he will do so without being pushed.

Thus Piaget's celebrated pessimism reduces to a conviction that the central objective of intervention should be maximal development and that acceleration may not be the best approach to that objective. It is also significant that his statement both begins ("so far incapable of proving") and ends ("needs a great deal of research") with a call for further study.

Further study has not yet provided a direct answer to the question, "What, if any, kind of intervention effects a maximal development?" Experimental studies *have* shown (1) that, with young children at least, "telling" methods, by themselves, produce quick but superficial results and (2) that methods based on equilibration theory (see the section on *Teaching: Principles* in this chapter) do effect limited but fundamental and lasting changes under certain conditions. The prerequisite for every student is attainment of a stage of development very close to the

---

*He goes on to say that time spent in "hatching an idea," in "simply going around in circles," makes the idea "more stable and fruitful in the long run."[59]

one to which the teaching sequence and the measurement procedure have been directed. If a student is already in transition between the Preoperational and Concrete Operational periods, for example, a very brief intervention can bring him firmly into Concrete Operations; but if before the intervention is he *early* Preoperational, the same intervention will not be successful. (See the earlier discussions of "sequential integration" and of "optimal discrepancy.") If the intervention is done during the transitional stage, the child will not only make a "correct" response (e.g., a "conservation" response: "They are the same.") but will explain how he arrived at his conclusion, will transfer it to different problems of the same type, and will resist all efforts to deceive him (as, for example, when the experimenter surreptitiously removes material from one of the objects or sets of objects in a conservation experiment).[61] Since he was not able to meet all those criteria before the intervention, it does appear that intervention can be an agent of change.

This experimental evidence comes from studies of interventions that have been extremely limited in both time and scope—days, hours, or even minutes, often dealing with but a single task. A question naturally arises concerning the possible effect of more extensive interventions over longer periods of time. Careful longitudinal studies are lacking, but there is a body of evidence concerning a closely related question: "What is the effect of a *culture* on the development of operational intelligence?" The answer seems to be that if observed differences in test performance between peoples from different cultures can be attributed to cultural differences, the effect is substantial. There are many hazards in cross-cultural research, but one of the worst —the frequently changing of tests from one study to another— has been reduced* in Piagetian research, not so much by design as by the predictable tendency of Piagetian psychologists to use Piagetian tests. In a review of recent (1958–1972) studies of

---

*It has been reduced, but not eliminated. A thorough analysis of "problems in research on culture and thought" can be found in a paper of that name by Jacqueline Goodnow.[62]

this kind, Dasen[63] reports that in some societies there are normal individuals who have not reached the stage of concrete operations even by the age of twelve (an age at which three-fourths of Piaget's early Genevan sample were into *formal* operations), and some investigators have found *no* formal thinking *at all* in the cultures they have studied.* Dasen comments with respect to formal operations that although there are too few studies to support a firm conclusion, it does appear that some cultures do not nurture formal thinking. With respect to concrete operations, he concludes that

> . . . in all cultures studied so far, some or all individuals reach the stage of concrete operations, although usually at a later age than middle-class Europeans. The fact, however, that some individuals, even of adult age, continue to show a pre-operational type of reasoning, and that some qualitative differences are being reported, indicates that environmental factors may be more important than Piaget seemed to hypothesize in his earlier writings.[64]

On the other hand, the cross-cultural studies reveal a stronger relationship between logical thinking and contact with western urban culture than they do between logical thinking and traditional schooling.[65] It may be that logical thinking is more functional in industrialized societies than in others and that "contact with western urban culture" engages children to some extent in the enterprises of those industrialized societies.

If so, the main function of schooling may be to refine and deepen that involvement.

---

*The category "cross-cultural studies" includes comparisons of socioeconomic classes within a single industrialized society. In the United States, development is slower in the lower classes than in the general population.

NOTES

[1]Constance K. Kamii and Rheta DeVries, "Piaget for Early Education," *in* R. K. Parker (ed) *The Preschool in Action*, 2nd ed. (Boston: Allyn & Bacon). In press.

[2]A very concise description of Kohlberg's stages may be found in L. Kohlberg and Phillip Whitten, "Understanding the Hidden Curriculum," *Learning*, December, 1972. For more thorough discussions, read some of the other Kohlberg publications listed in the bibliography of this book.

[3]Jean Piaget, quoted by Eleanor Duckworth, "Piaget Rediscovered," *in* R. E. Ripple and V. N. Rockcastle (eds.), *Piaget Rediscovered*, a section of *Journal of Research in Science Teaching*, vol. 2, 1964.

[4]Ruth Moss, "Child's Play: Piaget's Way to Knowledge," *Chicago Tribune,* Thursday, January 3, 1974.

[5]Marianne Denis-Prinzhorn, Constance Kamii, and Pierre Mounoud, "Pedagogical Applications of Piaget's Theory," *People Watching*, vol. 1, 1972, p. 69.

[6]Constance K. Kamii, "Evaluation of Learning in Preschool Education: Socio-emotional, Perceptual-Motor, and Cognitive Development," *in* Benjamin J. Bloom, Thomas Hastings, and George Madaus, *Handbook on Formative and Summative Evaluation of Student Learning* (New York: McGraw-Hill Book Co.), 1971.

[7]Constance K. Kamii and Rheta DeVries, "Piaget for Early Education," *in* R. K. Parker, *The Preschool in Action* (New York: Allyn & Bacon).

[8]The term was coined by L. Kohlberg and R. Mayer in "Development as the Aim of Education." *Harvard Educational Review*, 1972, vol. 42, pp. 449–498.

[9]Kamii and DeVries, "Piaget for Early Education."

[10]*Ibid.*

[11]*Ibid.*

[12]Jean Piaget, *Science of Education and the Psychology of the Child*, trans. Derek Coltman (New York: Orion), 1970.

[13]Jerome S. Bruner, "Nature and Uses of Immaturity," *American Psychologist*, vol. 27, pp. 7–9.

[14]Kamii and DeVries, "Piaget for Early Education."

[15]*Ibid.*

[16]*Ibid.*

[17]*Ibid.*

[18]*Ibid.*

[19]*Ibid.*

[20]*Ibid.*

[21]*Ibid.*

[22]*Ibid.*

[23]*Ibid.*

[24]*Ibid.*

[25]John W. Renner, Don G. Stafford, William J. Coffia, Donald H. Kellogg, and M. C. Weber, "An Evaluation of the Science Curriculum Improvement Study," *Science and Mathematics*, April 1973, p. 313.

[26]Compare pp. 32–34 with pp. 106–121 in John W. Renner and Don G. Stafford, *Teaching Science in the Secondary Schools* (New York: Harper and Row), 1972.

[27]*Ibid.*, pp. 107–112.

[28]*Ibid.*, pp. 114–116.

[29]*Ibid.*, p. 116.

[30]*Ibid.*, pp. 142ff and 147ff.

[31]*Ibid.*, pp. 147ff.

[32]*Ibid.*, p. 149.

[33]*Ibid.*

[34]*Ibid.*, p. 150.

[35]Joe W. McKinnon and John W. Renner, "Are Colleges Concerned with Intellectual Development?," *American Journal of Physics*, vol. 39, pp. 1047–1052; John W. Renner and Don G. Stafford, *Teaching Science in the Secondary Schools*, Appendix A, pp. 291ff; John W. Renner and Anton E. Lawson "Promoting Intellectual Development Through Science Teaching." *The Physics Teacher*, vol. 11, pp. 273–276.

[36]Elizabeth F. Karplus and Robert Karplus, "Intellectual Development Beyond Elementary School. I. Deductive Logic," *School Science and Mathematics*, May 1970, pp. 398–406; Robert Karplus and Rita W. Peterson, "Intellectual Development Beyond Elementary School. II. Ratio—A Survey." *School Science and Mathematics*, December 1970, pp. 813–820; Robert Karplus and Elizabeth F. Karplus, "Intellectual Development Beyond Elementary School. III. Ratio—A Longitudinal Study," *School Science and Mathematics*, November 1972, pp. 735–742; Lawrence Kohlberg and Carol Gilligan, "The Adolescent as a Philosopher—The Discovery of the Self in a Postconventional World," *Daedalus*, 1971, pp. 1051–1084; Kenneth Lovell, "Some Problems Associated With Formal Thought and its Assessment," *in* Donald Ross Green, Marguerite P. Ford, and George B. Flamer (eds.), *Measurement and Piaget*, Proceedings of the CTB/McGraw-Hill Conference on Ordinal Scales of Cognitive Development (New York: McGraw-Hill Book Co.), 1971; R. P. Tisher, "A Piagetian Questionnaire Applied to Pupils in a Secondary School," *Child Development*, vol. 42, 1971, pp. 1633–1636.

[37]Monique Laurendeau and Adrien Pinard, *Causal Thinking in the Child: a Genetic and Experimental Approach* (New York: International Universities Press), 1962; Adrien Pinard and Monique Laurendeau "A Scale of Mental Development Based on the Theory of Piaget," *Journal of Research in Science Teaching*, vol. 2, 1964, pp. 253–260; Monique Laurendeau and Adrien Pinard, *The Development of the Concept of Space in the Child* (New York: International Universities Press), 1970.

[38]Pinard and Laurendeau, "A Scale of Mental Development Based on the Theory of Piaget," p. 257.

[39]Personal communication from Professor Pinard, January 30, 1974.

[40]M. L. Goldschmid and P. M. Bentler, "The Dimensions and Measurement of Conservation," *Child Development*, 1968, vol. 39, pp. 787–802; A. S. Kaufman, "Piaget and Gesell—A Psychometric Analysis of Tests Built From Their Tasks," *Child Development*, vol. 42, 1971, pp. 1341–1360; E. A. Lunzer, "Construction of a Standardized Battery of Piagetian Tests to Assess the Development of Effective Intelligence," *Research in Education*, vol. 3, 1970, pp. 53–72; Read D. Tuddenham, "Theoretical Regularities and Individual Idiosyncrasies," *in* Donald Ross Green, Marguerite P. Ford, and George B. Flamer eds.), *Measurement and Piaget*, Proceedings of the CTB/McGraw-Hill Conference on Ordinal Scales of Cognitive Development (New York: McGraw-Hill Book Co.), 1971, pp. 64–80.

[41]A. S. Kaufman and N. L. Kaufman, "Tests Built From Piaget's and Gesell's Tasks as Predictors of First-grade Achievement," *Child Development*, vol. 43, 1972, pp. 521–535.

[42]F. W. Warburton, "The British Intelligence Scale," *in* W. B. Dockrell (ed.), *On Intelligence*, The Toronto Symposium on Intelligence (London: Methuen), 1969.

[43]Lawrence Kohlberg and Rheta DeVries, "Relations Between Piaget and Psychometric Assessments of Intelligence." Paper presented at the Conference on the Natural Curriculum of the Child, Urbana, Illinois, 1969; W. Beth Stephens, C. K. Miller, and J. A. McLaughlin, *The Development of Reasoning, Moral Judgment, and Moral Conduct in Retardates and Normals*. Report on Project No. RD-2382-P. Philadelphia, Pennsylvania: Temple Univ., May 1969; Elliott Ross, *An Investigation of Verbal and Nonverbal Expression of Reading Comprehension Skills and Classification Abilities at the Concrete Operations Stage*. Unpublished dissertation, Philadelphia, Pennsylvania: Temple Univ., 1971; C. E. Meyers and R. E. Orpet, "Ability Factor Location of some Piagetian Tasks at $5\frac{1}{2}$ Years," *Proceedings of the 79th Annual Convention of the American Psychological Association*, 1971; W. Beth Stephens, C. K. Miller, and J. A. McLaughlin, "Factorial Structure of Selected Psycho-educational Measures and Piagetian Reasoning Assessments," *Developmental Psychology*, vol. 6, 1972; Walter E. Hathaway, Anneke Hathaway-Theunissen, *The Unique Contributions of Piagetian Measurement to Diagnosis, Prognosis, and Research of Children's Mental Development*. Fourth Annual Conference on Piaget and the Helping Professions, Los Angeles, Calif., February 15, 1974.

[44]K. Lovell and I. B. Butterworth, "Abilities Underlying the Understanding of Proportionality," *Mathematics Teaching*, vol. 37, 1966, pp. 5–9.

[45]E. D. Dulit, "Adolescent Thinking *a la* Piaget—The Formal Stage," *Journal of Youth and Adolescence*, vol. 1, 1972; Elizabeth F. Friot, "The Relationship Between the Inquiry Teaching Approach and Intellectual Development." Ph.D. Dissertation, University of Oklahoma, 1970; Karplus and Karplus, "Intellectual Development Beyond the Elementary School. I: Deductive Logic," pp. 398–406; Karplus and Peterson, "Intellectual Development Beyond the Elementary School. II: Ratio— A Survey," pp. 813–820; McKinnon and Renner, "Are Colleges Concerned with Intellectual Development?," pp. 1047–1052; R. J. Ross, "Some Empirical Parameters of Formal Thinking," *Journal of Youth and Adolescence*, vol. 2, 1973, pp. 167–177.

[46]Friot, "The Relationship Between the Inquiry Teaching Approach and Intellectual Development," p. 402.

[47]Karplus and Peterson, "Intellectual Development Beyond the Elementary School. II. Ratio—A Survey," pp. 1048–1049.

[48]Jean Piaget, "Intellectual Evolution from Adolescence to Adulthood," *Human Development*, vol. 15, 1972, p. 6.

[49]Pierre R. Dasen, "Cross-cultural Piagetian Research—A Summary," *Journal of Cross-cultural Psychology*, vol. 3, 1972, pp. 23–39.

[50]John H. Flavell, *The Developmental Psychology of Jean Piaget* (New York: Van Nostrand Co., Inc.), 1963, p. 21.

[51]*Ibid.*, pp. 9–10.

[52]*Ibid.*, pp. 368–369.

[53]Norman E. Gronlund, *Determining Accountability for Classroom Instruction* (New York: Macmillan), 1974.

[54]The phrase was coined by Eleanor Duckworth, "The Having of Wonderful Ideas," *Harvard Educational Review*, vol. 42, 1972.

[55]David P. Ausubel, "Reception versus Discovery Learning in Classroom Instruction," *Educational Theory*, vol. 2, 1961, p. 21.

[56]*Ibid.*, p. 21.

[57]*Ibid.*, p. 21.

[58]Unpublished lecture at New York University, March 21, 1967. My source is a typescript in English, courtesy of a personal communication by Dr. Frank G. Jennings. Dr. Jennings makes no claim of precision, and Piaget has not approved the translation.

[59]From the same lecture; same source.

[60]From the same lecture; same source.

[61]An especially illuminating analysis of intervention effects may be found in Siegfried E. Englemann, "Does the Piagetian Approach Imply Instruction?" and in Constance K. Kamii and Louise Derman, "The Englemann Approach to Teaching Logical Thinking—Findings from the Administration of some Piagetian Tasks," *in* Donald Ross Green, Marguerite P. Ford, and George B. Flamer, *Measurement and Piaget* (New York: McGraw-Hill Book Co.), 1971.

[62]Jacqueline J. Goodnow, "Problems in Research on Culture and Thought," *in* David Elkind and John L. Flavell (eds.), *Studies in Cognitive Development— Essays in Honor of Jean Piaget* (New York: Oxford Univ. Press), 1969, pp. 439–462.

[63]Dasen, "Cross-cultural Piagetian Research—A Summary," pp. 23–40.

[64]*Ibid.*, pp. 23–40.

[65]*Ibid.*, p. 35.

Bibliography

This Bibliography is intended as a reading list for those students who are motivated to extend their study of Piaget's theory beyond the boundaries that I set for myself when writing this book. Because I assume that most of my readers are fluent only in English, I have cited only the translated version of any contribution that appeared originally in another language. The translated works of Piaget and his co-workers are listed chronologically according to the publication dates of the French editions.

Piaget's studies on perception and on the development of moral ideas in children are related to those on intellectual development, and someday all may be combined into an integrated theory of cognition; but anyone wishing to inquire into all of them will need to supplement the readings listed here.

Almy, M., E. Chittenden, and P. Miller. *Young Children's Thinking—Studies of Some Aspects of Piaget's Theory.* New York: Teachers College Press, 1966.

Alpert, D., and D. L. Bitzer. "Advances in Computer-based Education," *Science,* vol. 167, 1970, pp. 1582–1590.

Athey, Irene J., and Duane O. Rubadeau. *Educational Implications of Piaget's Theory.* Waltham, Mass.: Ginn-Blaisdell, 1970.

Ausubel, David P. "Reception versus Discovery Learning in Classroom Instruction." *Educational Theory,* vol. II, 1961, pp. 21–24.

Beard, R. M., "The Order of Concept Development Studied in Two Fields. I. Number Concepts in the Infants' School." *Educational Review,* vol. 15, pp. 105–117.

Bearison, David J. "Role of Measurement Operations in the Acquisition of Conservation." *Developmental Psychology,* vol. 1, 1969, pp. 653–660.

Beilin, H., and I. C. Franklin. "Logical Operations in Area and Length Measurement: Age and Training Effects." *Child Development,* vol. 33, 1962, pp. 607–618.

Beilin, H., J. Kagan, and R. Rabinowitz. "Effects of Verbal and Perceptual Training on Water-level Representation." *Child Development,* vol. 37, 1966, pp. 317–330.

Bereiter, Carl. "Educational Implications of Kohlberg's Cognitive-Developmental View." *Interchange,* vol. 1, 1970, pp. 25–32.

Beth, E. W., and Jean Piaget. *Mathematical Epistemology and Psychology,* trans. by Wolfe Mays. New York: Gordon and Breach, 1966. [Original French edition, 1961.]

Berzonsky, Michael D. "Interdependence of Inhelder and Piaget's Model of Logical Thinking." *Developmental Psychology,* vol. 4, 1971, pp. 469–476.

Birch, H. G. "The Relation of Previous Experience to Insightful Problem Solving." *Journal of Comparative Psychology,* 1945, pp. 367–383.

Bitzer, Donald L., and J. A. Easley, Jr. *Plato—A Computer-controlled Teaching System* (Symposium on Computer Augmentation of Human Reasoning). Washington, D.C.: Spartan Books, Inc., 1965, pp. 89–103.

Bloom, Benjamin S., J. Thomas Hastings, and George F. Madaus. *Handbook on Formative and Summative Evaluation of Student Learning.* New York: McGraw-Hill Book Co., 1971.

Bower, T. G. R. "The Visual World of Infants." *Scientific American,* vol. 215, no. 6 (December 1966), pp. 80–92. [Offprint 502]

———— "Phenomenal Identity and Form Perception in an Infant," *Journal of Perception and Psychophysics,* 1967, pp. 74–76.

Braine, M. D. S. "The Ontogeny of Certain Logical Operations: Piaget's Formulation Examined by Nonverbal Methods." *Psychological Monographs,* vol. 73, no. 5, 1959. Whole no. 475.

———— "Piaget on Reasoning: a Methodological Critique and Alternative Proposals," in W. Kessen and C. Kuhlman (eds.), "Thought in the Young Child." *Monograph Soc. Res. Child Development,* vol. 27 (2, Serial No. 83), 1962, pp. 41–61.

———— "Development of a Grasp of Transitivity of Length: A Reply to Smedslund." *Child Development,* vol. 35, 1964, pp. 799–810.

Braine, Martin D. S., and Betty L. Shanks. "The Development of Conservation of Size." *Journal of Verbal Learning and Verbal Behavior*, vol. 4, 1965, pp. 227–242.

Brainerd, Charles J., and Susan H. Brainerd. "Order of Acquisition of Number and Quantity Conservation." *Child Development*, vol. 43, 1972, pp. 1901–1906.

Brison, D. W. "Acceleration of Conservation of Substance." *Journal of Genetic Psychology*, vol. 109, 1966, pp. 311–322.

Bruner, Jerome S. *Process of Education*, New York: Vintage Books, 1960.

—— "The Course of Cognitive Development." *American Psychologist*, vol. 19, 1964, pp. 1–16.

—— "The Growth of Mind." *American Psychologist*, vol. 20, 1965, pp. 1007–1017.

—— *Toward a Theory of Instruction*. Cambridge: Harvard Univ. Press, 1966.

—— *Processes of Cognitive Growth in Infancy:* Heinz Werner Lectures, Clark University, Worcester (vol. 3), Barre, Massachusetts: Barre Publishers, 1968.

Bruner, Jerome S., R. R. Olver, P. M. Greenfield. *Studies in Cognitive Growth*. New York: John Wiley & Sons, Inc., 1966.

Bruner, Jerome S. "Nature and Uses of Immaturity." *American Psychologist*, vol. 27, 1972.

—— "The Organisation of Early Skilled Action," *in* M. P. Richards (ed.) *The Integration of the Child into a Social World*. New York: Cambridge Univ. Press, 1974.

Bynum, Terrell Ward, James A. Thomas, and Lawrence J. Weitz. "Truth-functional Logic in Formal Operational Thinking—Inhelder and Piaget's Evidence." *Developmental Psychology*, vol. 7, 1972, pp. 129–132.

Carey, Susan, and Ned Block. "Should Philosophy and Psychology Remarry?" *Contemporary Psychology*, vol. 18, 1973, pp. 597–600. [A review of *Cognitive Development and Epistemology*, ed. Theodore Mischel, Academic Press, 1971.]

Carini, Louis. "Symbolic Transformations Theorem on Language Learning" (reprint). *Proceedings 77th Annual Convention American Psychological Association*, 1969.

Case, Duncan, and J. M. Collinson. "The Development of Formal Thinking in Verbal Comprehension." *British Journal of Educational Psychology*, vol. 57, 1962, pp. 103–111.

Cole, Michael, John Gay, Joseph A. Glick, and Donald W. Sharp. *The Cultural Context of Learning and Thinking—An Exploration in Experimental Anthropology*. New York: Basic Books, 1971.

Cowan, Philip A., Jonas Langer, Judith Heavenrich, and Marjorie Nathanson. "Social Learning and Piaget's Cognitive Theory of Moral Development." *Journal of Personality and Social Psychology*, vol. 11, 1969, pp. 261–274.

Dasen, Pierre R. "Cross-Cultural Piagetian Research—A Summary." *Journal of Cross-Cultural Psychology*, vol. 3, 1972, pp. 23–39.

Decarie, Therese Gouin. *Intelligence and Affectivity in Early Childhood: An Experimental Study of Jean Piaget's Object Concept and Object Relations*, Translation by P. Brandt and L. W. Brandt. New York: International Universities Press, 1966.

Dennis-Prinzhorn, Marianne, Constance Kamii, and Pierre Mounoud. "Pedagogical Application of Piaget's Theory." *People Watching*, vol. 1, 1972.

Dockrell, W. B. (ed.). *On Intelligence* (The Toronto Symposium on Intelligence). London: Methuen, 1969.

Dodwell, P. C. "Children's Understanding of Number and Related Concepts." *Canadian Journal of Psychology*, vol. 14, 1960, pp. 191–205.

———— "Children's Understanding of Number Concepts; Characteristics of an Individual and of a Group Test." *Canadian Journal of Psychology*, vol. 15, 1961, pp. 29–36.

———— "Relations Between the Understanding of the Logic of Classes and of Cardinal Number in Children." *Canadian Journal of Psychology*, vol. 16, 1963, pp. 152–160.

Duckworth, Eleanor. "The Having of Wonderful Ideas." *Harvard Educational Review*, vol. 42, 1972.

———— "Piaget Takes a Teacher's Look." *Learning*, vol. 2, 1973, pp. 22–27.

Dudek, S. Z., E. P. Lester, J. S. Goldberg, and G. B. Dyer. "Relationship of Piaget Measures to Standard Intelligence and Motor Scales." *Perceptual and Motor Skills*, vol. 28, 1969, pp. 351–362.

Dulit, E. D. "Adolescent Thinking *a la* Piaget—The Formal Stage." *Journal of Youth and Adolescence*, vol. 1, 1972, pp. 281–301.

Easley, J. A., Jr. "The Structural Paradigm in Protocol Analysis. *Journal of Research in Teacher Education* (in press).

———— and Klaus G. Witz. "Individualized Instruction—Some Observations from the Ivory Tower." *Educational Technology*, vol. 14, 1974.

Educational Testing Service. *Instructional and Assessment Materials for First Graders—Manual of Directions*. New York: Board of Education of the City of New York, 1965.

———— *Let's Look at First Graders—A Guide to Understanding and Fostering Intellectual Development in Young Children* (rev. ed.). New York: Board of Education of the City of New York, 1965.

———— *Written Exercises for First Graders—Manual of Directions*. New York: Board of Education of the City of New York, 1965.

Elkind, David. "Giant in the Nursery—Jean Piaget." *New York Times Magazine*, May 26, 1968, pp. 25–27 and 50–57.

———— "The Development of Quantitative Thinking: A Systematic Replication of Piaget's Studies." *Journal of Genetic Psychology*, vol. 98, 1961, pp. 37–46.

———— "Children's Discovery of the Conservation of Mass, Weight, and Volume: Piaget Replication Study II." *Journal of Genetic Psychology*, vol. 98, 1961, pp. 219–227.

———— "The Development of the Additive Composition of Classes in the Child: Piaget Replication Study III." *Journal of Genetic Psychology*, vol. 99, 1961, pp. 51–57.

—— "Children's Conception of Right and Left: Piaget Replication Study IV." *Journal of Genetic Psychology*, vol. 99, 1961, pp. 269–276.

—— "Children's Conception of Brother and Sister: Piaget Replication Study V." *Journal of Genetic Psychology*, vol. 100, 1962, pp. 129–136.

—— "Discrimination, Seriation, and Numeration of Size and Dimensional Differences in Young Children: Piaget Replication Study VI." *Journal of Genetic Psychology*, vol. 104, 1964, pp. 275–296.

Elkind, David, and John Flavell. *Studies in Cognitive Development: Essays in Honor of Jean Piaget*. New York: Oxford Univ. Press, 1969.

Elkind, David. "Measuring Young Minds—Piaget." *Horizon*, Winter 1971.

—— Elkind, David. *Children and Adolescents—Interpretive Essays on Jean Piaget* (2nd ed.). New York: Oxford Univ. Press, 1974.

Featherstone, Joseph. *Schools Where Children Learn*. New York: Liveright, 1971.

Feffer, M., and L. Suchotliff. "Decentering Implications of Social Interactions." *Journal of Personality and Social Psychology*, vol. 4, 1966, pp. 415–442.

Festinger, L. *A Theory of Cognitive Dissonance*, Evanston. Illinois: Row, Peterson, 1957.

Flavell, John H. *The Developmental Psychology of Jean Piaget*. Princeton: D. Van Nostrand Co., Inc., 1963.

Freyberg, P. S. "Concept Development in Piagetian Terms in Relation to School Attainment." *Journal of Educational Psychology*, vol. 57, 1966, pp. 164–168.

Friot, Faith Elizabeth. "The Relationship Between the Inquiry Teaching Approach and Intellectual Development." (Ph.D. dissertation, University of Oklahoma, 1970.)

Furth, H. G. "Conservation of Weight in Deaf and Hearing Children." *Child Development*, vol. 35, 1964, pp. 143–150.

—— *Thinking Without Language—Psychological Implications of Deafness*. New York: The Free Press, 1966. London: Collier-Macmillan Ltd. (2nd printing), 1968.

—— "Piaget's Theory of Knowledge—The Nature of Representation and Interiorization." *Psychological Review*, vol. 75, 1968, pp. 143–154.

—— *Piaget and Knowledge—Theoretical Foundations*. Englewood Cliffs, New Jersey: Prentice-Hall, 1969.

—— *Piaget for Teachers*. Englewood Cliffs, New Jersey: Prentice-Hall, 1970.

Furth, H. G., and Harry Wachs. *Thinking Goes to School—Piaget's Theory in Practice*. New York: Oxford Univ. Press, 1974.

Furth, H. G., James Youniss, and Bruce M. Ross. "Children's Utilization of Logical Symbols—An Interpretation of Conceptual Behavior Based on Piagetian Theory." *Developmental Psychology*, vol. 3, 1970, pp. 36–57.

Furth, H. G., and James Youniss. "Formal Operations and Language—A Comparison of Deaf and Hearing Adolescents." *International Journal of Psychology*, vol. 6, 1971, pp. 49–64.

Gagné, R. M. "The Acquisition of Knowledge." Psychological Review, vol. 69, 1962, pp. 355–365.

—— *The Conditions of Learning*. New York: Holt, Rinehart and Winston, 1965.

—— "Curriculum Research and the Promotion of Learning," in *Perspectives of Curriculum Evaluation*, AERA Monograph Series on Curriculum Evaluation, no. 1. Chicago: Rand-McNally, 1967, pp. 19–38.

—— "Contributions of Learning in Human Development." *Psychological Review*, vol. 75, 1968, pp. 177–191.

—— "Learning Hierarchies." Presidential address to Division 15, American Psychological Association, August 31, 1968.

—— *Essentials of Learning for Instruction*. Hinsdale, Illinois: The Dryden Press, 1974.

Gagné, R. M., and L. T. Brown. "Some Factors in the Programming of Conceptual Learning." *Journal of Experimental Psychology*, vol. 62, 1961, pp. 313–331.

Gagné, R. M., J. R. Mayor, H. L. Garstens, and N. E. Paradise. "Factors in Acquiring Knowledge of a Mathematical Task." *Psychological Monographs*, vol. 76, no. 526, 1962.

Gagné, R. M., and N. E. Paradise. "Abilities and Learning Sets in Knowledge Acquisition." *Psychological Monographs*, vol. 75, no. 518, 1961.

Gelman, Rochel. "Conservation Acquisition—A Problem of Learning to Attend to Relevant Attributes." *Journal of Experimental Psychology*, vol. 7, 1969, pp. 167–187.

—— "The Nature and Development of Early Number Concepts," in *Advances in Child Development and Behavior*. New York: Academic Press, 1972, pp. 116–167.

Gilmary, Sister I. H. M. "Examination of Some of Piaget's Principles in Application to Psychology of Arithmetic." *Catholic Educational Review*, vol. 62, 1964, pp. 369–375.

Goldschmid, Marcel L., and P. M. Bentler. *Concept Assessment Kit—Conservation, Manual*. San Diego: Educational and Industrial Testing Service, 1968.

—— "The Dimensions and Measurement of Conservation." *Child Development*, vol. 39, 1968, pp. 787–802.

Goodnow, Jacqueline J. "A Test of Milieu Effects with Some of Piaget's Tasks." *Psychological Monographs*, vol. 76, no. 36, 1962.

—— "Problems in Research on Culture and Thought," *in* David Elkind and John H. Flavell (eds.) *Studies in Cognitive Development*. New York: Oxford Univ. Press, 1969, pp. 439–462.

—— and Gloria Bethon. "Piaget's Tasks—The Effects of Schooling and Intelligence." *Child Development*, vol. 37, 1966, pp. 573–582.

Gratch, Gerald, Kenneth J. Appel, Wilson F. Evans, Guney K. LeCompte, and Nancy A. Wright. "Piaget's Stage IV Object Concept Error—Evidence of Forgetting or Object Conception?" *Child Development*, vol. 45, 1974, pp. 71–77.

Griffiths, Judith, Carolyn Shantz, and I. E. Sigel. "A Methodological Problem in Conservation Studies: The Use of Relational Terms." *Child Development*, vol. 38, no. 3, 1967, pp. 841–848.

Gronlund, Norman E. *Determining Accountability for Classroom Instruction*. Macmillan, 1974.

Gruen, G. E. "Experiences Affecting the Development of Number Conservation in Children." *Child Development*, vol. 36, 1965, pp. 964–979.

Hall, Elizabeth. "A Conversation with Jean Piaget." *Psychology Today*, May 1970.

Harlow, H. F. "The Formation of Learning Sets." *Psychological Review*, vol. 56, 1949, pp. 51–65.

Hebb, D. O. *The Organization of Behavior*. New York: John Wiley & Sons, Inc., 1949.

———— *A Textbook of Psychology*. Philadelphia: W. B. Saunders Co., 1958 (1st ed.), 1966 (2nd ed.)

Hill, Barry. "Piaget Now" (Parts 1 to 3). London: *The London Times Educational Supplement*, February 11, 18, and 25, 1972.

High/Scope Educational Research Foundation. *The High/Scope Early Elementary Program—Cognitively Oriented Curriculum for Project Follow-Through, Grades K–3*. Ypsilanti, Michigan: High/Scope Educational Research Foundation, 1973.

———— *Early Childhood Education and Research—Report 1973*. Ypsilanti, Michigan: High/Scope Educational Research Foundation, 1974.

Hogan, Robert. "Moral Conduct and Moral Character—A Psychological Perspective." *Psychological Bulletin*, vol. 79, 1973, pp. 217–232.

Hood, H. Blair. "An Experimental Study of Piaget's Theory of the Development of Number in Children." *British Journal of Psychology*, vol. 53, no. 3, 1962. pp. 273–286.

Hunt, J. McV. *Intelligence and Experience*. New York: Ronald Press Co., 1961.

———— "Piaget's Observations as a Source of Hypotheses Concerning Motivation." *Merrill-Palmer Quarterly*, vol. 9, 1963, pp. 263–275.

Inhelder, Bärbel. "Criteria of the Stages of Mental Development," *in* J. M. Tanner and Barbel Inhelder (eds.). *Discussions on Child Development*, New York: International Universities Press, 1953.

———— "Operational Thought and Symbolic Imagery," *in* P. H. Mussen (ed.), *European Research in Cognitive Development*, *Monographs of the Society for Research in Child Development*, vol. 30, no. 2, 1965, pp. 4–18.

———— *Diagnosis of Reasoning in the Mentally Retarded* (trans. Will Beth Stephens). New York: John Day, 1968.

Inhelder, Bärbel, M. Bovet, Hermina Sinclair, and C. D. Smock. "On Cognitive Development." *American Psychologist*, vol. 21, 1966, 160–165.

Inhelder, Bärbel, and Jean Piaget. *Diagnosis of Reasoning in the Mentally Retarded*, trans. by W. B. Stephens. New York: John Day, 1968. [Original French edition, 1943.]

———— *The Early Growth of Logic in the Child: Classification and Seriation*. New York: Harper and Row, Publishers, Inc., 1964. [Original French edition, 1959.]

———— *The Growth of Logical Thinking from Childhood to Adolescence: An Essay on the Construction of Formal Operational Structures*, translated by Anne Parson and S. Milgram. New York: Basic Books, 1958. [Original French edition 1955.]

Inhelder, Bärbel, and Hermina Sinclair. "Learning Cognitive Structures," *in* Paul H. Mussen, Jonas Langer, and Martin Covington (eds.) *Trends and Issues in Developmental Psychology*. New York: Holt, Rinehart and Winston, 1969, pp. 2–21.

Irwin, Michelle D., and G. Shirley Moore. "The Young Child's Understanding of Social Justice." *Developmental Psychology*, vol. 5, 1971, pp. 406–410.

Jahoda, G. "Child Animism. I. A Critical Survey of Crosscultural Research. II. A Study in West Africa." *Journal of Social Psychology*, vol. 47, pp. 197–222.

Kamii, Constance K. "Piaget's Theory and Specific Instruction—A Response to Bereiter and Kohlberg." *Interchange*, vol. 1, 1970.

———— "Evaluation of Learning in Preschool Education—Socioemotional, Perceptual-motor, and Cognitive Development," *in* Benjamin S. Bloom, J. Thomas Hastings, and George F. Medaus (eds.) *Handbook of Formative and Summative Evaluation of Student Learning*. New York: McGraw-Hill Book Co., 1971, pp. 284–344.

———— "An Application of Piaget's Theory to the Conceptualization of a Preschool Curriculum," *in* R. K. Parker (ed.) *The Preschool in Action*. Boston: Allyn and Bacon, 1972.

———— "A Sketch of the Piaget-derived Preschool Curriculum Developed by the Ypsilanti Early Education Program," *in* S. Braun and E. Edwards (eds.) *History and Theory of Early Childhood Education*. Worthington, Ohio: Jones, 1972. [Also available in J. Frost (ed.) *Revisiting Early Childhood Education*, B. Spodek (ed.) *Early Childhood Education*, and J. Torrey (ed.) *The Prepared Tearcher*.]

Kamii, Constance K., and Rheta DeVries. "Piaget for Early Education," *in* R. K. Parker (ed.) *The Preschool in Action*. Boston: Allyn and Bacon (in press).

Kamii, Constance K., and N. L. Radin. "A Framework for a Preschool Curriculum Based on Some Piagetian Concepts." *Journal of Creative Behavior*, vol. 1, 1967, pp. 314–324.

———— "A Framework for a Preschool Curriculum Based on Piaget's Theory," *in* I. J. Athey and D. O. Rubadeau (eds.) *Educational Implications of Piaget's Theory*. Waltham, Mass.: Ginn-Blaisdell, 1970, pp. 89–100.

Karplus, Elizabeth F., and Robert Karplus. "Intellectual Development Beyond Elementary School. I. Deductive Logic." *School Science and Mathematics*, May 1970, pp. 398–406.

Karplus, Robert, and Elizabeth F. Karplus. "Intellectual Development Beyond Elementary School. III. Ratio—A longitudinal Study." *School Science and Mathematics*, November 1972, pp. 735–742.

Karplus, Robert, and Rita W. Peterson. "Intellectual Development Beyond Elementary School. II. Ratio—A Survey." *School Science and Mathematics*, December 1970, pp. 813–820.

Kaufman, A. S. "Piaget and Gesell—A Psychometric Analysis of Tests Built from Their Tasks." *Child Development*, vol. 42, 1971, pp. 1341–1360.

―――― and N. L. Kaufman. "Tests Built from Piaget's and Gesell's Tasks as Predictors of First-grade Achievement." *Child Development*, vol. 43, 1972, pp. 521–535.

Kendler, Tracy S. "Development of Mediating Responses in Children." *Monographs of Society of Research in Child Development*, vol. 28, 1963, pp. 33–48.

Kephart, Newell C. *The Slow Learner in the Classroom.* Columbus, Ohio: Charles E. Merrill Books, Inc., 1960.

―――― *Learning Disability.* West LaFayette, Indiana: Kappa Delta Pi Press, 1968.

Knifong, J. D. "Logical Abilities of Young Children—Two Styles of Approach." *Child Development*, vol. 45, 1974, pp. 78–83.

Kofsky, E. "A Scalogram Study of Classificatory Development." *Child Development*, vol. 37, 1966, pp. 191–204.

Kohlberg, Lawrence.

―――― "The Child as a Moral Philosopher." *Psychology Today*, September 1968.

―――― "Early Education—A Cognitive-Developmental View." *Child Development*, vol. 39, 1968, pp. 1013–1062.

―――― and Rheta DeVries.

Kohlberg, Lawrence, and Carol Gilligan. "The Adolescent as a Philosopher—The Discovery of the Self in a Postconventional World." *Daedalus*, vol. 100, 1971, pp. 1051–1084.

Kohlberg, Lawrence, and C. Lesser.

Kohlberg, Lawrence, and R. Mayer. "Development as the Aim of Education." *Harvard Educational Review*, vol. 42, 1972, pp. 449–498.

Kohlberg, Lawrence, and Phillip Whitten. "Understanding the Hidden Curriculum." *Learning*, December 1972, pp. 9–19.

Kohler, Wolfgang. *The Mentality of Apes* (1924), translated from second revised edition by Ella Winter. New York: Vintage Books, 1959.

Kohnstamm, G. A. "An Evaluation of Part of Piaget's Theory." *Acta Psychologica*, vol. 1, 1963, pp. 313–356.

Kuhn, Deanna. "Mechanisms of Change in the Development of Cognitive Structures." *Child Development*, vol. 43, 1972, pp. 833–844.

Kuhn, T. S. "The Function of Measurement in Modern Physical Science," in H. Woolf (ed.) *Quantification.* Indianapolis: Bobbs-Merrill, 1961.

L'Abate, L. "Consensus of Choice Among Children—A Test of Piaget's Theory of Cognitive Development." *Journal of Genetic Psychology*, vol. 100, 1962, pp. 143–149.

Lambie, Dolores Z., James T. Bond, and David P. Weikart. *Infants, Mothers and Teachering—A Stody of Infant Education and Home Visits* (Summary of Final Report, Ypsilanti Carnegie Infant Education Project). Ypsilanti, Michigan: High/Scope Educational Research Foundation, 1974.

Langer, Jonas. "Disequilibrium as a Source of Development," in P. H. Mussen, J. Langer, and M. Covington (eds.) *Trends and Issues in Developmental Psychology.* New York: Holt, Rinehart and Winston, Inc. 1969, pp. 22–37.

———— and Sidney Strauss. "Appearance, Reality, and Identity." *Cognition*, vol. 1, 1972, pp. 105–128.

Laurendeau, Monique, and Adrien Pinard. *Causal Thinking in the Child—A Genetic and Experimental Approach.* New York: International Universities Press, 1962.

———— The Development of the Concept of Space in the Child. New York: International Universities Press, 1970.

Lavatelli, C. *Early Childhood Curriculum—A Piaget Program.* Boston: American Science and Engineering, 1970.

———— *Teacher's Guide to Accompany Early Childhood Curriculum—A Piaget Program.* Boston: American Science and Engineering, 1970.

———— *A Piaget Preschool Program in Action* (Parts I and II, Number, Measurement, and Space). Little Neck, New York: Knowledge Tree Films, 1971.

Looft, William R., and Wayne H. Bartz. "Animism Revisited." *Psychological Bulletin*, vol. 71, 1969, pp. 1–19.

Lovell, K. "A Follow-up Study of Some Aspects of the Work of Piaget and Inhelder on the Child's Conception of Space." *British Journal of Educational Psychology*, vol. 29, 1959, pp. 104–117.

———— "A Follow-up Study of Inhelder and Piaget's 'The Growth of Logical Thinking.' " *British Journal of Psychology*, vol. 52, 1961, pp. 143–153.

———— The Growth of Basic Mathematical and Scientific Concepts in Children. London: Univ. London Press, 1961.

Lovell, K., B. Mitchell, and I. R. Everett. "An Experimental Study of the Growth of Some Logical Structure." *British Journal of Psychology*, vol. 53, no. 2, 1962, pp. 175–188.

Lovell, K., and A. Slater. "The Growth of the Concept of Time: A Comparative Study." *Journal of Child Psychology and Psychiatry*, vol. 1, 1960, pp. 179–190.

Lubin, Gerald I., James F. Magary, and Marie K. Paulsen. *Piagetian Theory and the Helping Professions—Proceedings of the Second Interdisciplinary Seminar on Piagetian Theory and Its Implications for the Helping Professions* (1972). Educational Resources Information Center (Office of Education), 1973.

———— *Piagetian Theory and the Helping Professions—Proceedings of the Third Interdisciplinary Seminar on Piagetian Theory and Its Implications for the Helping Professions* (1973). Educational Resources Information Center (Office of Education), 1974.

———— *Piagetian Theory and the Helping Professions—Proceedings of the Fourth Interdisciplinary Seminar on Piagetian Theory and Its Implications for the Helping Professions* (1974). Los Angeles: University of Southern California, 1975.

Lunzer, E. A. "Some Points of Piagetian Theory in Light of Experimental Criticism." *Journal of Child Psychology and Psychiatry*, vol. 1, 1960, pp. 191–200.

———— *Recent Studies in Britain Based on the Work of Jean Piaget.* London: National Foundation of Educational Research in England and Wales, 1960.

———— "Construction of a Standardized Battery of Piagetian Tests to Assess the Development of Effective Intelligence." *Research in Education*, vol. 3, 1970, pp. 53–72.

McKinnon, Joe W., and John W. Renner. "Are Colleges Concerned with Intellectual Development?" *American Journal of Physics*, vol. 39, 1971, pp. 1047–1052.

Moss, Ruth. "Child's Play—Piaget's Way to Knowledge." *Chicago Tribune*, January 3, 1974.

———— "The Games Children Play Could Be Life's Lessons." *Chicago Tribune*, January 5, 1974.

Murray, Frank. "Cognitive Conflict and Reversibility Training in the Acquisition of Length Conservation." *Journal of Educational Psychology*, vol. 59, 1968, pp. 82–87.

Nolen, Patricia. "Piaget and the School Psychologist."

O'Bryan, K. G., and R. S. MacArthur. "A Factor Analytic Study of Piagetian Reversibility." *Alberta Journal of Educational Research*, vol. 13, 1967, pp. 211–220.

Ojemann, R. H., and Karen Pritchett. "Piaget and the Role of Guided Experiences in Development." *Perception and Motor Skills*, vol. 17, 1963, pp. 927–940.

Peel, E. A. "Experimental Examination of Some of Piaget's Schemata Concerning Children's Perceptions and Thinking, and a Discussion of their Educational Significance." *British Journal of Educational Psychology*, vol. 29, no. 2, 1959, pp. 89–103.

Piaget, Jean. *The Language and Thought of the Child*, translated by Marjorie Worden. New York: Harcourt, Brace & World, Inc., 1926. [Original French edition, 1923.]

———— *Judgment and Reasoning in the Child*, translated by Marjorie Worden. New York: Harcourt, Brace & World, Inc., 1928. [Original French edition, 1924.]

———— *The Child's Conception of the World*, translated by Joan and Andrew Tomlinson. New York: Harcourt, Brace & World, Inc., 1929. [Original French edition, 1926.]

———— *The Child's Conception of Physical Causality*, translated by Marjorie Worden. New York: Harcourt, Brace & World, Inc., 1930 [Original French edition, 1927.]

———— *The Moral Judgment of the Child*, translated by Marjorie Worden. New York: Harcourt, Brace & World, Inc., 1932.

———— *The Origins of Intelligence in Children*, translated by Margaret Cook. New York: International Universities Press, 1952. [Original French edition, 1936.]

———— *The Construction of Reality in the Child*, translated by Margaret Cook. New York: Basic Books, Inc., 1954. [Original French edition, 1937.]

———— *Play, Dreams, and Imitation in Childhood*, translated by C. Gattegno and F. M. Hodgson. New York: W. W. Norton & Co., Inc., 1951. [Original French edition, 1945.]

—— *The Child's Conception of Movement and Speed*, trans. by G. E. T. Holloway and M. J. Mackenzie. London: Routledge & Kegan Paul Ltd., 1970. [Original French edition, 1946.]

—— *The Child's Conception of Time*, trans. by A. J. Pomerans. London: Routledge & Kegan Paul Ltd., 1969. [Original French edition, 1946.]

—— *The Psychology of Intelligence*, translated by M. Piercy and D. E. Berlyne. London: Routledge & Kegan Paul Ltd., 1950 [Original French edition, 1947.]

—— "Jean Piaget," *in* E. G. Boring, H. S. Langfeld, H. Werner, and R. M. Yerkes (eds.). *A History of Psychology in Autobiography*, Worcester, Massachusetts: Clark University Press, 1952.

—— "How Children Form Mathematical Concepts." *Scientific American*, vol. 189, no. 5 (November 1953), pp. 74–79. [Offprint 420]

—— "The Development of Time Concepts in the Child," *in* R. H. Hoch and J. Zubin (eds.). *Psychopathology of Childhood*, New York: Grune & Stratton, Inc., 1955.

—— *Logic and Psychology* (based on lectures delivered at the University of Manchester, England, in 1952), New York: Basic Books, Inc., 1957.

—— "The Child and Modern Physics." *Scientific American*, vol. 196, no. 3 (March 1957), pp. 46–51.

—— "Development and Learning." *Journal of Research in Science Teaching*, vol. 2, 1964, pp. 176–186.

—— *Six Psychological Studies* (edited by David Elkind). New York: Random House, Inc., 1967.

—— *Biology and Knowledge*. Chicago: The Univ. of Chicago Press, 1971. [Original French edition, 1967.]

—— *On the Development of Memory and Identity:* Heinz Werner Lectures, Clark University, Worcester (vol. 2). Barre, Massachusetts: Barre Publishers, 1967.

—— *Structuralism*, trans. by Chaninah Maschler. New York: Basic Books, 1971. [Original French edition, 1968.]

—— *Science of Education and the Psychology of the Child*, trans. by Derek Coltman. New York: Orion Press, 1970. [From two essays completed in 1935 and 1969.]

—— *Genetic Epistemology*, trans. by Eleanor Duckworth. New York: Columbia Univ. Press, 1970. [Original French edition, 1970.]

—— *The Principals of Genetic Epistemology*, trans. by Wolfe Mays. London: Routledge & Kegan Paul Ltd., 1972. [Original French edition, 1970.]

—— *Psychology and Epistemology*, trans. by Arnold Rosin. New York: Grossman, 1971. [Original French edition, 1970.]

—— *Mental Imagery in the Child—A Study of the Development of Imaginal Representation*, trans. by P. A. Chilton. New York: Basic Books, 1971. [Original French edition, 1966.]

—— *To Understand is To Invent—The Future of Education*. New York: Grossman, 1973. [A Translation of two works written for UNESCO in 1948 and 1971.]

———— *The Child and Reality—Problems of Genetic Psychology*. New York: Viking Press, 1973. [Original French edition, 1972.]

Piaget, Jean, and Bärbel Inhelder. "Diagnosis of Mental Operations and Theory of Intelligence." *American Journal of Mental Deficiency*, vol. 51, no. 3, 1947, pp. 401–406.

———— *The Child's Conception of Space*, translated by F. J. Langdon and J. L. Lunzer. London: Routledge & Kegan Paul Ltd., 1956. [Original French edition, 1948.]

———— *Psychology of the Child*, trans. by Helen Weaver. London: Routledge & Kegan Paul Ltd., 1969. [Original French edition, 1967.]

———— "The Gaps in Empiricism," *in* A. Koestler (ed.) *Beyond Reductionism*. New York: Hutchinson, 1969, pp. 118–148.

———— *Memory and Intelligence*, trans. by Arnold J. Pomerans. New York: Basic Books, 1972. [Original French edition, 1968.]

Piaget, Jean, Bärbel Inhelder, and Alina Szeminska. *The Child's Conception of Geometry*, translated by E. A. Lunzer. New York: Basic Books, Inc., 1960. [Original French edition, 1948.]

Piaget, Jean, and Alina Szeminska. *The Child's Conception of Number*, translated by C. Gattegno and F. M. Hodgson. New York: Humanities Press, Inc., 1952. [Original French edition, 1941.]

Pinard, Adrien, and Monique Laurendeau. "A Scale of Mental Development Based on Piaget's Theory." *Journal of Research in Science Teaching*, vol. 2, 1964, pp. 253-260.

———— " 'Stage' in Piaget's Cognitive-Developmental Theory—Exigesis of a Concept," *in* David Elkind and John H. Flavell (eds.) *Studies in Cognitive Development—Essays in Honor of Jean Piaget*. New York: Oxford Univ. Press, 1969.

Renner, John W., Judith Brock, Sue Heath, Mildred Laughlin, and Jo Stevens. "Piaget IS Practical." *Science and Children*, October 1971, pp. 23–26.

———— and Anton E. Lawson. "Piagetian Theory and Instruction in Physics." The Physics Teacher, vol. 11, 1973, p. 165.

———— "Promoting Intellectual Development Through Science Teaching." *The Physics Teacher*, vol. 11, 1973, pp. 273–276.

Renner, John W., and Donald G. Stafford. "Inquiry, Children, and Teachers." *The Science Teacher*, April 1970, pp. 55–57.

———— *Teaching Science in the Secondary School*. New York: Harper & Row, 1972.

Renner, John W., Donald G. Stafford, William J. Coffia, Donald H. Kellogg, and M. C. Weber. "An Evaluation of the Science Curriculum Improvement Study." *School Science and Mathematics*, April 1973, pp. 291–318.

Ripple, R. E., and V. N. Rockcastle (eds.). "Piaget Rediscovered: Selected Papers from a Conference on Cognitive Studies and Curriculum Development." *Journal of Research in Science Teaching*, vol. 2, no. 3, 1964.

Ross, Robert J. "Some Empirical Parameters of Formal Thinking." *Journal of Youth and Adolescence*, vol. 2, 1973, pp. 167–177.

———— "The Empirical Status of the Formal Operations." *Adolescence*, vol. 9, 1974, pp. 413–420.

Schwebel, Milton, and Jane Raph. *Piaget in the Classroom*. New York: Basic Books, 1973.

Sigel, Irving E. "Developmental Trends in the Abstraction Ability of Children." *Child Development*, vol. 24, 1953, pp. 131–144.

———— "The Attainment of Concepts," *in* M. L. Hoffman and Lois V. Hoffman, *Review of Child Development Research*. New York: Russell Sage Foundation, vol. 1, 1964, pp. 209–248.

Sigel, Irving E., and Frank H. Hooper. *Logical Thinking in Children: Research Based on Piaget's Theory*. New York: Holt, Rinehart and Winston, Inc., 1968.

Sigel, Irving E., Annemarie Roeper, and Frank H. Hooper. "A Training Procedure for Acquisition of Piaget's Conservation of Quantity: A Pilot Study and its Replication." *British Journal of Educational Psychology*, vol. 36, 1966, pp. 301–311. (Reprinted in Irving E. Sigel and Frank H. Hooper, *Logical Thinking in Children: Research Based on Piaget's Theory*, New York: Holt, Rinehart and Winston, Inc., 1968.)

Sigel, Irving E., E. Saltz, and W. Roskind. "Variables Determining Concept Conservation." *Journal of Experimental Psychology*, vol. 7, 1967, pp. 471–475.

Slobin, Dan I. "Cognitive Prerequisite for the Development of Grammar," *in* Charles A. Ferguson and Dan Issac Slobin (eds.). *Studies of Child Language Development*. New York: Holt, Rinehart and Winston, 1973, pp. 175–208.

Smedslund, Jan. "The Acquisition of Conservation of Substance and Weight in Children: I. Introduction." *Scandinavian Journal of Psychology*, vol. 2, 1961, pp. 11–20.

———— "The Acquisition of Conservation of Substance and Weight in Children: II. External Reinforcement of Conservation of Weight and the Operations of Additions and Subtractions." *Scandinavian Journal of Psychology*, vol. 2, 1961, pp. 71–84.

———— "The Acquisition of Conservation of Substance and Weight in Children: III. Extinction of Conservation of Weight Acquired 'normally' and by Means of Empirical Controls on a Balance." *Scandinavian Journal of Psychology*, vol. 2, 1961, pp. 85–87.

———— "The Acquisition of Conservation of Substance and Weight in Children: IV. Attempt at Extinction of the Visual Components of the Weight Concept." *Scandinavian Journal of Psychology*, vol. 2, 1961, pp. 153–155.

———— "The Acquisition of Conservation of Substance and Weight in Children: V. Practice in Conflict Situations Without External Reinforcement." *Scandinavian Journal of Psychology*, vol. 2, 1961, pp. 156–160.

———— "The Acquisition of Conservation of Substance and Weight in Children: VI. Practice on Continuous vs. Discontinuous Material in Problem Situations Without External Reinforcement." *Scandinavian Journal of Psychology*, vol. 2, 1961, pp. 203–210.

—— "The Acquisition of Conservation of Substance and Weight in Children: VII. Conservation of Discontinuous Quantity and the Operations of Adding and Taking Away." *Scandinavian Journal of Psychology*, vol. 3, 1962, pp. 69–77.

—— "The Effect of Observation on Children's Representation of the Spatial Orientation of a Water Surface." *Journal of Genetic Psychology*, vol. 102, 1963, pp. 195–201.

—— "Development of Concrete Transitivity of Length in Children." *Child Development*, vol. 34, 1963, pp. 389–405.

—— "Concrete Reasoning—A Study of Intellectual Development." *Monographs of the Society for Research in Child Development*, vol. 29, no. 2, ser. 93, 1964, pp. 1–39.

—— "The Development of Transitivity of Length—A Comment on Braine's Reply." *Child Development*, vol. 36, 1965, pp. 577–580.

Sonquist, H., and Constance K. Kamii. "Applying Some Piagetian Concepts in the Classroom for the Disadvantaged." *Young Children*, vol. 22, 1967, pp. 231–246.

—— and L. Derman. "A Piaget-derived Preschool Curriculum," *in* I. Athey and D. Rubaeau (eds.) *Educational Implications of Piaget's Theory.* Waltham, Mass.: Ginn-Blaisdell, 1970.

Stephens, W. Beth, Charles K. Miller, and John A. McLaughlin. *The Development of Reasoning, Moral Judgment, and Moral Conduct in Retardates and Normals.* Report on Project No. RD-2382-P, Philadelphia, Penn.: Temple Univ., 1969.

Stephens, W. Beth, John A. McLaughlin, Charles K. Miller, and Gene V. Glass. "The Factorial Structure of Reasoning, Moral Judgment, ·and Moral Conduct." *Developmental Psychology*, vol. 6, 1962.

Strauss, Sidney, and Jonas Langer. "Operational Thought Inducement." *Child Development*, vol. 41, 1970, pp. 163–175.

Suchman, J. Richard. "The Illinois Studies in Inquiry Training." *Journal of Research in Science Teaching*, vol. 2, 1964, pp. 231–232.

Szeminska, Alina. "The Evolution of Thought: Some Applications of Research Findings to Educational Practice," *in* P. H. Mussen (ed.) *European Research in Cognitive Development, Monographs of the Society for Research in Child Development*, vol. 30, no. 2, 1965, pp. 47–57.

Tanner, J. M., and Bärbel Inhelder (eds.). *Discussions on Child Development: A Consideration of the Biological, Psychological, and Cultural Approaches to the Understanding of Human Development and Behavior* (volume Four of *The Proceedings of the World Health Organization Study Group on the Psychobiological Development of the Child, Geneva, 1956*). New York: International Universities Press, 1960.

Tisher, R. P. "A Piagetian Questionnaire Applied to Pupils in a Secondary School." *Child Development*, vol. 42, pp. 1633–1636.

Tuddenham, Read D., "Jean Piaget and the World of the Child." *American Psychologist*, vol. 21, March 1966, pp. 207–217.

Turiel, Elliot. "An Experimental Test of the Sequentiality of Developmental Stages in the Child's Moral Judgments." *Journal of Personality and Social Psychology*, vol. 3, 1966, pp. 611–618.

────── and Golda R. Rothman. "The Influence of Reasoning on Behavioral Choices at Different Stages of Moral Development." *Child Development*, vol. 43, 1972, pp. 741–756.

Tynum, Terrell Ward, James A. Thomas, and Lawrence J. Weitz. "Truth-functional Logic in Formal Operational Thinking—Inhelder and Piaget's Influence." *Developmental Psychology*, vol. 7, 1972, pp. 129–132.

Uzgiris, Ina C. "Situational Generality of Conservation." *Child Development*, vol. 35, 1964, pp. 831–841.

Vernon, P. E. "Environmental Handicaps and Intellectual Development." *British Journal of Educational Psychology*, vol. 35, 1965, pp. 9–20, 117–126.

────── "Educational and Intellectual Development Among Canadian Indians and Eskimos." *Educational Review*, vol. 18, 1966, pp. 79–91, 186–195.

Wallach, Lise, A. Jack Wall, and Lorna Anderson. "Number Conservation: the Roles of Reversibility, Addition-Subtraction, and Misleading Perceptual Cues." *Child Development*, vol. 38, 1967, pp. 425–442.

Wallach, Lise, and R. L. Sprott. "Inducing Number Conservation in Children." *Child Development*, vol. 35, 1964, pp. 1057–1071.

Warburton, F. W. "The British Intelligence Scale," *in* W. B. Dockrell (ed.) *On Intelligence* (The Toronto Symposium on Intelligence). London: Methuen, 1969.

Watson, John S., and Gary Danielson. "An Attempt to Shape Bidimensional Attention in 24-Month-Old Infants." *Journal of Experimental Child Psychology*, vol. 7, 1969, pp. 467–478.

Weikart, D., L. Rogers, C. Adcock, and D. McClelland. *The Cognitively Oriented Curriculum—A Framework for Preschool Teachers*. Urbana, Illinois: Univ. of Illinois Press, 1971.

White, Burton L. "An Experimental Approach to the Effects of Experience on Early Human Behavior," *in* J. P. Hill (ed.), *Minnesota Symposium on Child Psychology* (vol. 1). Minneapolis: Univ. of Minnesota Press, 1967, pp. 201–225.

────── and Richard Held. "Plasticity of Sensorimotor Development in the Human Infant," *in* Judy F. Rosenblith and W. Alinsmith (eds.), *The Causes of Behavior: Readings in Child Development and Educational Psychology* (2nd ed.). Boston: Allyn and Bacon, Inc., 1966.

White, Sheldon H. "Evidence for a Hierarchical Arrangement of Learning Processes." *Advances in Child Development and Behavior*, vol. 2, 1965, pp. 187–220.

Wohwill, Joachim F. "Developmental Studies of Perception." *Psychological Bulletin*, vol. 57, 1960, pp. 249–288.

────── "A Study of the Development of the Number Concept by Scalogram Analysis." *Journal of Genetic Psychology*, vol. 97, 1960, pp. 345–377.

────── "Piaget's System as a Source of Empirical Research." *Merrill-Palmer Quarterly*, vol. 9, 1963, pp. 253–262.

———— "Cognitive Development and the Learning of Elementary Concepts." *Journal of Research in Science Teaching*, vol. 2, 1964, pp. 222, 226.

———— "Comments in Discussion on the Developmental Approach of Jean Piaget." *American Journal of Mental Deficiency, Monograph Supplement*, vol. 70, 1966, pp. 84–105.

———— "Piaget's Theory of the Development of Intelligence in the Concrete Operations Period." *American Journal of Mental Deficiency, Monograph Supplement*, vol. 70, 1966, pp. 57–83.

———— "The Mystery of the Prelogical Child." *Psychology Today*, vol. 1, 1967, pp. 25–34.

Wohlwill, Joachim F., and R. C. Lowe. "Experimental Analysis of the Development of the Conservation of Number." *Child Development*, vol. 33, 1962, pp. 153–168.

Wolfe, Peter H. "The Developmental Psychologies of Jean Piaget and Psychoanalysis." *Psychological Issues*, vol. II, 1960.

Woodward, Mary. "The Behavior of Idiots Interpreted by Piaget's Theory of Sensori-Motor Development." *The British Journal of Educational Psychology*, vol. 29, February 1959, pp. 60–71.

———— "Concepts of Number of the Mentally Subnormal Studied by Piaget's Method." *Journal of Child Psychology and Psychiatry*, 1961, pp. 249–259.

———— "Concepts of Space in the Mentally Subnormal Studied by Piaget's Method." *British Journal of Social and Clinical Psychology*, vol. 1, 1962, pp. 25–37.

Youniss, James, Hans G. Furth, and Bruce M. Ross. "Logical Symbol Use in Deaf and Hearing Children and Adolescents." *Developmental Psychology*, vol. 5, 1971, pp. 511–517.

Zimiles, H. "The Development of Differentiation and Conservation of Number." *Monograph Society for Research in Child Development*, vol. 31, no. 6, 1966. Whole no. 108.

Index

The names of authors listed in the Notes at the end of each chapter are not included in this index unless they also appear in the text.